CHAIM
GROSS

1. MOTHER PLAYING. 1961. Bronze, 48 × 80″. Hadassah-Hebrew University Medical Center, Jerusalem. Gift of Mr. and Mrs. Morris Primoff, New York City

CHAIM GROSS

by Frank Getlein

HARRY N. ABRAMS, INC., PUBLISHERS, NEW YORK

MARGARET L. KAPLAN, *Managing Editor*
NAI Y. CHANG, *Creative Director*
RUTH EISENSTEIN, *Editor*
THOMAS LINCOLN, *Book Design*
LISA PONTELL, *Picture Editor*

designed by Thomas Lincoln

Library of Congress Cataloging in Publication Data

GROSS, CHAIM, 1904–
    Chaim Gross.
    Bibliography: p.
    1. Gross, Chaim, 1904–   I. Getlein, Frank.
NB237.G85G47   730'.92'4   73–13807
ISBN 0–8109–0160–9

Library of Congress Catalogue Card Number: 73–13807
Published by HARRY N. ABRAMS, INCORPORATED, *New York 1974*
Printed and bound in Japan

CONTENTS

LIST OF PLATES

CHAIM GROSS

OUT FROM THE CENTER OF JERUSALEM, in a spectacular landscape of steeply rising heights and deep valleys, there stands, among the Judean hills, the modern and constantly growing Hadassah-Hebrew University Medical Center. In a small area of grass and walks in front of the Center's Mother and Child Pavilion, set on a pedestal, is a bronze sculpture of a half-reclining woman balancing a little girl on her leg—*Mother Playing* by Chaim Gross. The woman's figure describes a long, low horizontal arc and looks as if, given a push, it would rock back and forth.

Somewhat under life size, the graceful bronze figure is familiar and accessible to the many children who play on the grass while they wait for parents visiting inside. The bow of the rocking mother implies, as Gross's figures often do, a much larger arc, even a complete circle, of which the figure is only a segment. Set upon this bow, the child's form balances the raised head of the mother. Supported by the timeless grace of the arc, mother and child rise above it, assert their individuality, not so much against as within the endless, or eternal, form upon which they rest in their joy of each other. (The self-sufficient, closed, completed form is a frequent motif in Gross's sculpture; in works in which it is not dominant, often the principal force lines, if continued in the mind's eye, trace a circle invisible to the outward eye but obviously pres-

ent to the sculptor's vision.) In the bright sunlight of Israel, the infinitely faceted bronze of the *Mother Playing* reflects the gleams and glints of that light at every angle. To walk around the piece is to follow a continually shifting light pattern upon its surface. The solid bronze is enduring at once by virtue of its substance and, paradoxically, by virtue of this light play, in which its very substance seems to be dissolved.

The theme of the happy mother and child recurs continually in Gross's work, and the reasons can be no great mystery. For one thing, he and his wife have raised a son and a daughter, the latter an extraordinarily happy artist, as is abundantly clear to those who know the paintings of Mimi Gross. The work of the younger artist is worlds removed from the sculpture of the older, but the playful, happy, exuberant spirit that characterizes her work is also the sustaining force behind most of his. And there is another reason why the theme of the happy mother appears and reappears in the world of Chaim Gross. He began his life in the warm atmosphere implied in that theme, then saw his private paradise shattered, brutally destroyed before his eyes, by the vast impersonal forces of international conflict, while he himself, a child forced into precocious maturity, was driven out of that youthful Eden into an alien and often hostile world. The *Mother Playing*, in

2. The artist at home with his wife, Renee, their son, Yehudah,
and their daughter, Mimi. 1944

Gross's vision, is at one time a memory, an act of grateful homage,
and the expression of a passionate desire for the happiness of all
mothers and children.

Taken together with its location, the *Mother Playing* comes as
close as any work could to summing up the life and achievement
of its author. The setting could not be more appropriate to Gross's
vision, allegiances, and aspirations. The very landscape is a kind of
abstract symbolic setting of a citadel attained in the face of great
peril. The citadel is of course the State of Israel, and the peril is
the entire history of that state, for that matter the entire history
of the Jewish people for some nineteen hundred years before the
establishment—or reestablishment—of Israel. And the Hadassah
medical enterprise itself has a history in miniature not unlike that
of Israel. It had been opened in 1939 on Mount Scopus in the Old
City of Jerusalem but was evacuated during the 1948 war (the War
of Independence). After the end of that war Mount Scopus remained an Israeli enclave behind Jordan lines until the Six-Day
War of 1967 liberated the Old City and reunified Jerusalem. Today the Mount Scopus units are being rebuilt and expanded; in the
meantime, the Hadassah-Hebrew University Center had been established on the outskirts of the new city, where it has virtually
unlimited room for the expansion necessitated by advances in

medicine and by the steady rise of standards of medical care in
Israel. The story of the Center, then, like that of Israel, adds up to
a magnificent and expanding achievement based on opportunities
derived from what originally seemed tragic circumstances. In this,
both share a pattern of life with Chaim Gross.

Gross was born in Wolowa (Volovo), a tiny village in Austrian
Galicia, in 1904, on a day—March 17 (St. Patrick's Day)—that

3. The artist's mother and father. 1916

4. The artist
   at the age
   of thirteen

assures him, as it amuses him to affirm, of New York City's biggest annual parade being held every year on the anniversary of his birth. The village, situated in the heart of the Carpathian Mountains, had a population of ten families, which added up to a total population probably larger than that figure would imply today. In the Gross family, headed by Chaim's father, Moses Gross, a timber appraiser employed in the area's leading industry, there were ten children. The five eldest succumbed to the casual cruelty of nature, dying within a week in a diphtheria epidemic a few years before Chaim was born; he thus grew up hearing about brothers and sisters he had never known. He was the youngest of the surviving five, including one sister and three brothers. No doubt childhood influences on an artist can be overemphasized, but it is a fact that Chaim Gross grew up with wood in his earliest years. He still remembers the summers when he tagged along while his father surveyed lumber stands in the countryside and the long, cold winters when whittling figures and forms in wood was a favorite indoor pastime of family and friends.

When Chaim was seven, his father decided that the children needed more schooling than was available in the remote village of Wolowa. He moved his family to Kolomyya, a town of some thirty thousand inhabitants, whose name combines the Ukrainian words for "washing" and "wheel." The children now attended secular school and *cheder* (religious school). The family adhered to the Hasidic branch of Judaism, in which joyousness is emphasized— "happy people, very pious, people who believed in making other people happy," the sculptor testifies.

The happiness did not last long. Chaim was ten when, in 1914, the power struggles of Europe erupted into his life and destroyed all that he had known. At the very beginning of World War I the Imperial Russian troops invaded Galicia and occupied Kolomyya,

killing, looting, and raping at random. The Gross house was a little way outside the town; shortly after midnight, the first day of the invasion, the Cossacks arrived, tore the door off, and plundered the house of everything they considered valuable. Chaim saw them slashing with their sabers at his mother and father, who tried with bleeding hands to protect each other's heads. He and his brother Abraham fled through the night to a neighbor's; when they returned they found their father and mother unconscious on the floor. A long period passed in which the Austrian and German forces battled the Russians through and out of the town, inflicting more damage in each round. The schools, which had attracted Moses Gross to the town in the first place, closed, and in 1916 the family joined a general Jewish exodus from Kolomyya into the anonymous terrain of war and exile. The fugitives traveled on foot from one village to another. "The Russians were chasing us," Gross recalls vividly. "We were sleeping on roofs and in the fields, with the sound of cannon fire always in the distance." Eventually they came to "a larger city" (its name forgotten, or never known), and then "the government took care of us, bringing trains to take us farther into Austria, traveling westward away from the fighting." Gross remembers that during the train rides from town to town, whenever the train pulled into a station the townsfolk would bring hot soup and other food to the refugees. At one stop he got lost and missed the train, but a few days later he got on another train going in the same direction and quite by chance found his parents again in the city of Stry. After weeks of shuttling around in the Austro-Hungarian railway system, the family came to rest in Austrian Silesia, where the Hapsburg government had built "enormous barracks" for refugee families from the Eastern front. Weary with wandering, they settled in.

Not Chaim. As he remembers it, he was in Silesia barely a fortnight when he joined a group of boys his own age who had decided to set out for Vienna, the great metropolis, the capital of the entire world for children born and brought up in the Dual Monarchy. The little band reached its goal only to find that the Viennese were starving. Chaim and his brother Abraham, who had joined the expedition mainly because they thought their eldest brother, Pincus, was in Vienna, heard, after making inquiries, that he had moved on to Budapest, and they followed him down the Danube. In Budapest they stationed themselves on two separate

13

street corners in the center of town, and about five or six o'clock in the evening, they caught sight of him. "He was paralyzed and on crutches."

In Budapest the three brothers found that the anti-Semitism which had seemed to them a more or less normal feature of life in the Hapsburg realms was all but nonexistent. There were virtually no legal restrictions, and such anti-Jewish feeling as there was, manifested itself chiefly in the country districts. Chaim felt more at ease in Budapest than he had felt anywhere since leaving the little Carpathian village of Wolowa. He supported himself with odd jobs and began to pick up the craft of the gold- and silversmith. Lingering at a café table, he would draw idly on the stationery that was freely available under the old dispensation. "That's where my art began," he declares. "From that time on I drew more and more, until I sometimes sat all day copying pictures from magazines and filling the pages of sketchbooks."

The defeat suffered by the Central Powers in 1918 brought out the always strong Hungarian nationalist feeling, which led to what Chaim Gross remembers as the first of three revolutions in rapid succession—the coming to power of the Radical Socialists under Károlyi (November 1918). During his regime a new art school was opened, and young Chaim won a scholarship including room and board, the first objective evidence that his drawing in coffeehouses had not been a waste of time. Károlyi was not long for power however: the republic of Hungary was invaded by the Czechs, the Serbians, and the Rumanians, all reclaiming lands occupied by the Hapsburgs over the centuries. During this crisis the Communist Béla Kun, returning from Russia, where he had embraced Bolshevism, seized power (March 1919). The Kun government rapidly followed the path that was part of the Communist pattern under the new Soviet government—rule by terror (involving, incidentally, the abolition of the art school, Chaim's scholarship, and with it his room and board). The terror destroyed the school, but it did not keep the invading Rumanians from occupying and thoroughly looting the capital, a disaster that resulted in the end of the Kun government and the restoration of the monarchy under a "regent," Admiral Horthy. This counterrevolution brought to power the two most anti-Semitic elements in Hungarian life, the landowners and the military. As Jews and "foreigners," Abraham and Chaim were thrown into prison and then, after three months, deported

to Austria. In the same spirit the new Austrian republic deported them to Poland, since they had come to Budapest from what had in the meantime become Polish Silesia. The spirit of the time during which Chaim Gross was an adolescent is accurately rendered in that classic satire on war and the military bureaucracy, Jaroslav Hašek's *Good Soldier Schweik*. But at least Schweik was able to strike back at the local representatives of the high powers that were disrupting his life; the boy from Galicia was seized and helplessly tossed about as in a storm by the Czarist Russians, the Hapsburgs, the Hungarian Communists, Europe's first fascists, and the emerging anti-Semites of Austria, in that order.

Meanwhile the next to the eldest of the brothers, Naftoli, had made his way to America (where he later became well known as a lyric poet, writing in Yiddish), and he began sending his brothers money to help them emigrate. While waiting for his visa, the young artist went back to Vienna and enrolled in a trade school with an art department. After several months visas were received, and at last, on April 14, 1921, Chaim, now seventeen, and his brother Abraham arrived at Ellis Island.

Once again Chaim was involved in a great historic movement of peoples, the last substantial wave of United States immigration, which brought thousands of East European Jews, in the wake of the Irish and the Italians, to the Lower East Side of Manhattan. Following the pattern of the industrious immigrants around him, within a few days of his arrival Chaim got a job as delivery boy for a fruit and vegetable market at eight dollars a week. By the second week his own life pattern asserted itself: he enrolled in the art school of the Educational Alliance on East Broadway, a settlement house that was an enormously influential force in the cultural life of New York City. The urban art of twentieth-century America, begun early in the century by Henri, Sloan, Glackens, and Luks, was to take a different, and in some ways deeper, turn in the hands of immigrant artists, many of whom studied at the Educational Alliance Art School. The celebration of the city that these artists, especially Sloan, initiated was to become, in the years before World War II, a penetrating analysis of the pathos of the city and an eloquent plea for urban humanity. Gross's own work has only rarely articulated such attitudes explicitly, but he was surely influenced to a profound degree by the general concern with social amelioration that shaped the artistic and intellectual life of the

Alliance. He met there, among other young artists in training, Peter Blume, Adolph Gottlieb, and, above all, the Soyer brothers, Isaac, Moses, and Raphael, who became and have remained close friends.

The initial attraction of the Alliance was that the language of instruction was Yiddish, the lingua franca of the immigrant culture—and one of the many languages and sublanguages that Gross can still handle, others being Hebrew, Polish, German, Ukrainian, Hungarian, and Swabian. He remained at the Alliance for the next four years as a student; eventually he joined the teaching staff, and he has continued teaching there. Over the years he has added a class at the New School for Social Research, the remarkable institution that, in certain ways, is the grand culmination of the settlement-house educational approach. For many years teaching was an essential feature of Gross's personal economy, and it has always been a part of his philosophy that it is the duty of an artist to pass on, along with whatever he has invented for himself, the knowledge that he has received from others.

Chaim changed jobs in order to further his artistic training. He became a delivery boy—"first with a pushcart, then on a bicycle"—for a grocery store at Sixty-seventh Street and Amsterdam Avenue, then, as now, a neighborhood with its own art enclave. The salary was again eight dollars—apparently the going rate for delivery boys in the twenties—but he now received room and board as well, and he was able to arrange his working hours with his employer so that he could attend a drawing class at the Beaux-Arts Institute of Design in addition to continuing his studies at the Alliance. It was a full schedule. Bright, energetic, and willing, Chaim had to resist the efforts of the grocer to promote him to clerk: a delivery boy could accommodate his working hours to his classes, a clerk could not. More important, it seemed to this artist on wheels that a clerk would have to be involved with customers and with the stock, whereas a delivery boy, cycling about the West Side, could all the while be drawing in his head.

And not only drawing. A friend and fellow student named Leo Jackinson, after studying Chaim's drawings, pointed out to him, with what can now be recognized as keen penetration, that his real talent was for sculpture. The youth took the suggestion and studied modeling for five years, along with drawing. When he felt that he had learned about all he could from formal classes, he left

5. WEST SIDE GIRL.
1929.
Lignum vitae,
height 18".
Collection Alfred and
Shirley Goldis,
New York City

both schools and quit his job as well (1927). But he did enroll at the Art Students League for a month—"That's all I could afford"—to learn the rudiments of direct carving from Robert Laurent. "That was the beginning of my carving." He took a room on Fourteenth Street, furnished it with apple crates, a butter tub that he painted and used for a seat, and a mattress that Raphael Soyer gave him. Both artists were living from hand to mouth, working at odd jobs for a day or even for a few hours at a time. It was a depressing situation, and Soyer convinced Gross that they had to "do something to stop living like this." What they did was to master, in two weeks, the machine embroidery trade, an ancillary to the garment industry that was central to the economy of the Lower East Side. The regular money that their new activity brought in was welcome, but the hours and the nature of the work used up the time and energy that Chaim wanted to put into his art. Living frugally, he saved two hundred dollars and went back to odd jobs and carving.

Gross and the Soyers were at this time members of an informal group of art students and artists who met in the Ninth Street studio of Jack Friedland, a lithographer specializing in the twenty-four-sheet billboard posters used by circuses and movie houses, and the only one of the group who was making a decent living. Raphael and Chaim took their meals there through an arrangement whereby Friedland acquired Raphael's paintings. For the rest, Chaim sometimes had no other resources than the nickels he won playing

15

6. The artist with HAPPY MOTHER. 1931

chess at Friedland's. One Christmas season he went off to Atlantic City to get a job as a dishwasher in a hotel, leaving a discouraged good-bye note; his friends, knowing how bad things were with him, feared that he had committed suicide.

It is a grim commentary, as Gross has himself pointed out, that his rumored demise caused his first sale. A wealthy art collector, hearing the sad news, was stricken with remorse that he had not previously acquired any of Chaim's sculpture, which he had seen at the Downtown Gallery, on Thirteenth Street. To please the collector, two of Chaim's friends managed to get into his studio, and they sold the collector a sculpture in wood and two watercolors. When Chaim reappeared, after about two months, it was something of an anticlimax, since it caused the market value of his work to drop.

Still, the period was not without its redeeming features. Most important, the limitation of activities imposed by poverty enabled Chaim to work devotedly at carving his small pieces. He began, as students tend to do, with soft woods. But when, more or less

accidentally, he came by a piece of hard wood, he found, and knew he had found, his métier. "The mallet and chisel felt better in my hands. I needed the resistance of the hard woods and, later, of stone." Chaim began exhibiting at the Independents' annual show at the Hotel Astor—"For two dollars anyone could show anything"—and there made his second sale, to a Dr. Schneidman, a veterinarian, who paid off the fifty-dollar price in installments of three dollars a week.

Chaim was an early exhibitor at Edith Halpert's Downtown Gallery, one of the first New York galleries to handle contemporary American art, but the connection did not last. "One day I came in and saw a piece of mine being used as a doorstop!"

In the course of this Bohemian existence, the practice and the steady perfecting of his art sustained the young sculptor, but presently another source of sustenance came into his life. One night at Friedland's, while Chaim was absorbed in trying to win a few nickels at chess, a girl named Renee Nechin dropped in to visit one of the group. Now a student at the City College, Renee had, like Chaim, arrived in America from Eastern Europe. Her family had lived on the Polish-Russian border, and her father had fled to America to escape conscription. After four years he had managed to save enough to send for his family. At the age of eleven, Renee found herself, without a word of English, enrolled in the second grade in Fairfield, Connecticut, where her father had acquired a general store.

Renee came again. This time the whole crowd took a long walk on Second Avenue; conversation was general and lively. A few weeks later Renee dropped in again to talk and to look at the work, and after an interval she came once more. Her visits to the studio became fairly regular, and soon she and Chaim regarded themselves as "going together," in the parlance of the day. But there were troubles. First, there was no money at all. Second, another member of the group had given Renee's parents a bad impression of Chaim, and it did not help any that they all habitually referred to him as "the woodchopper." Still, if heaven gives signs of marriages made there, it appears, from the events of the wedding day, that their marriage was so favored. It was on a day in 1932 that Renee, watching Chaim "chipping away" in the studio, said, "Let's get married." They were on the way to City Hall before Chaim realized that neither of them had the two dollars for the license. At this critical moment a young woman friend happened along and lent Chaim the two dollars, a ring she had with her, and her own presence as a witness. After the ceremony, she invited the couple to her apartment for a wedding dinner and gave them half a dollar for two tickets to a movie. As was common during the Depression, the movie program was enhanced by a bingo game, and Chaim won fifteen dollars. "It was enough to live on for three weeks," he recalls, the sheer unexpected luck of the moment still alive for him more than forty years later.

As if that small bit of luck at the very start of his marriage marked a turn in his fortunes, Chaim Gross seemed to move into the Land of Promise so far as art was concerned. Once more he was being acted upon by historical forces, but this time they were working in his favor. At all financial levels of the American society, the collapse of the speculative boom of the late twenties led to the misery of the Depression in the early thirties. The New Deal took up the enormous task of patching the economy together again, turning its prime attention to getting people steady work and steady

7. HELEN TAMIRIS. 1934. Lignum vitae, height 40".
Formerly, James Monroe High School, Bronx, New York

pay. For most Americans the steady work and steady pay provided under the Works Progress Administration was a comedown from their accustomed standards, even a source of embarrassment—at best, a stopgap. For the American artist, however, the WPA Federal Art Project and related programs represented a turning point. For the first time the society seemed to become aware of its artists in all fields. It began to assist them as it was assisting all needy citizens. The government was subsidizing theater and music, history, photography, painting and sculpture. But the New Deal art projects went beyond the assumption of the basic responsibility for the subsistence of artists. The programs also served to create an audience for art such as had not existed before, and this was the foundation of the steadily growing appreciation of, and sophistication in, the arts that has marked American life since then. Art centers were opened in all parts of the country. In the new, and largely unwelcome, leisure resulting from the Depression, people began going to free art exhibitions as well as to free concerts and plays; from this experience derives most of the support for the arts that still exists on a broad base in America. The young, newly married sculptor was in on the new movement from the beginning and stayed in touch with "the Project" (the WPA art programs) from time to time throughout its life. When it was over, Chaim Gross, along with a whole generation of American artists, was confirmed in his art with a dedication and an intensity that might well not have been possible without the government programs.

The first of the government programs for the arts, sparked by the painter George Biddle, who was a friend of President Roosevelt, was the Public Works of Art Project. In New York the PWAP was run by the vigorous director of the Whitney Museum of American Art, Juliana Force. Gross was among the first artists to be signed on, receiving the top pay of $42.50 a week. His principal commission was a carved figure of the dancer Helen Tamiris for James Monroe High School in the Bronx. The PWAP served as a proving ground for government participation in the arts. It was soon superseded by two other programs: the Section of Painting and Sculpture of the Treasury Department, concerned with obtaining the best possible art work—usually by commission—for the new buildings the government was erecting in Washington and around the country as part of the New Deal's recovery plan; and the Art Program of the Works Progress Administration

8. BASKETBALL PLAYERS. 1934. Mahogany, height 54".
Abraham Lincoln High School, Brooklyn, New York

9. HIGH JUMP. 1934. Mahogany, height 54″.
Abraham Lincoln High School, Brooklyn, New York

10. The artist at work on ALASKAN MAIL CARRIER. 1936

of the Federal Works Agency, which was mainly concerned with applying the New Deal principle of work relief to artists. The basic salary was $23.75 plus tools and materials. Work that was the product of full-time employment became the property of the project. Two wood reliefs that Gross made, *High Jump* and *Basketball Players,* were installed in Abraham Lincoln High School, in Brooklyn, and are still there.

The "Project" was regarded by most of the artists of the period who had it in them to move beyond the subsistence work provided, as a kind of insurance, a basic minimum, a reliable source of steady work. The Section of Painting and Sculpture of the Treasury Department, directed by Edward Bruce, was quite another matter. Since it had as its sole objective the acquisition of art of the highest quality for the new government buildings, murals and reliefs (and to a certain extent freestanding sculptures) were of primary interest. One of the generally overlooked results of the Section's need for murals was the experience it provided artists in designing and painting on a large scale, an experience that was directly reflected in the new American painting that emerged after World War II. The first big operation of the Section was to commission art work for the new Department of Justice and Post Office Department buildings in Washington. The Section made its first selections through the combination of a country-wide poll of experts around the country and an open competition. Thirty-six sculptors competed in the final round, and Gross was one of twelve selected to execute their designs in full scale. His winning sculpture, *Alaskan Mail Carrier* (1936; cast aluminum), stood in the Postmaster General's office, along with a statue of Benjamin Franklin, the groundbreaking postmaster general of the Colonies, by William Zorach, who, like Gross, was a pioneer in reviving direct carving in twentieth-century American sculpture. The commission amounted to three thousand dollars.

In 1938 he won a second commission in the same amount; this was for a stone lintel piece for the Pennsylvania Avenue doorway of the offices of the Federal Trade Commission, the so-called Apex Building, completing the Federal Triangle, bounded by Constitution and Pennsylvania avenues and Fourteenth Street, an area in the original plan of Pierre L'Enfant, designer of the capital, but not completed until the advent of the New Deal. Four sculptors were employed on the building, among them Robert Laurent, who, a few years earlier at the Art Students League, had given Gross his first instruction in direct carving. The Fine Arts Section kept a sort of interlocking system going among its numerous outposts around the country. An immediate result of Gross's winning the competition for the FTC building was another commission, for a family group fourteen feet high, to be placed outside the French Pavilion in the New York World's Fair of 1939–40. Gross executed another work for the Fair's Court of Peace, the figure of a linesman, for the Finland building. Also from the Treasury network came a commission for a relief for the new Post Office building in

11. The artist at work on HARVEST. 1938–39

20

12. HARVEST. 1939. Plaster, height 14'. France Overseas Building, World's Fair, New York. 1939–40

Irwin, Pennsylvania. Irwin being part of the complex of small iron-and-steel towns around Pittsburgh, Gross created a relief of steel-mill puddlers, the workers who melt the pig iron and, almost like cooks skimming a stew, remove the impurities that float to the surface, in preparation for further treatment. At the World's Fair he became something of a public figure, for he was one of the artists commissioned by the New York WPA Art Project to demonstrate sculpture before the eyes of the millions of visitors. Throughout the summer of 1940 he was in his studio in the Fair's American Art Today Pavilion, making sketches, drawings, and studies and then

"chipping away" at a five-foot log that by the end of the season became the Brooklyn Museum's *Ballerina*.

During these years of the New Deal it was gradually realized by the art world of New York and of the country at large that Chaim Gross was making a highly individual and distinctive contribution to the emerging form of American sculpture. The two-man show in which he exhibited in 1935 at the Guild Art Gallery was characterized by Wayne Craven in *Sculpture in America* as "a daring exhibit of the work of two gifted and unknown sculptors— Chaim Gross and Ahron Ben-Shmuel, both advocates of direct

13. The artist at work on PUDDLERS. 1940

14. BALLERINA. 1940. Imbuya wood, height 53 1/8''.
The Brooklyn Museum, New York City

carving.'' His co-exhibitor, Ben-Shmuel, had learned stonecutting in a quarry, and all his best work was reminiscent of the blocky work done by stonecutters; he related, clearly, to such other direct stone carvers of the time as Zorach and Flanagan. Gross, working in wood, related to no one at all: an immigrant from Galicia, who had been in the country less than a decade and a half and still spoke with the inflection of his native tongue, or tongues, he emerged in that exhibition as an authentic American original.

From the point of view of medium, Gross was doing two new things. He was carving in wood, practicing an art that in the course of the nineteenth century had virtually vanished from Europe and America. On both continents the wood-carving technique lingered on in the whittling of objects of folk art—in Europe in such out of the way places as Galicia, the Black Forest, the Tyrol, and in this country in New England, the Midwest, and the cowboy terrain. In America there had been the carvers of ships' figureheads and related forms in the eighteenth and the early nineteenth century; there had been William Rush carving his allegorical figure of the Schuylkill River, as immortalized by Thomas Eakins. And then the medium had gone into eclipse. In Europe, of course, the tradition of wood carving was richer and deeper, including such Northern medieval artists as Veit Stoss and Riemenschneider and many of the masters of the Renaissance and Baroque periods. The tradition persisted well into the Rococo, for which it was in fact peculiarly appropriate, adaptable as it was to the elaborate decorative motifs evolved in that period for wall decoration and furniture embellishment. But again, from early in the nineteenth century there was a hiatus—up to Brancusi and Moore. Gross brought to life in modern America an old and fruitful tradition that had, for a variety of complex reasons, vanished from among the means and methods in the repertory of the sculptor.

As a direct carver, Gross was of course participating in a much broader revolution—the revolt against the academism that dominated American sculpture, as it dominated sculpture in Europe. There have always been two basic ways to produce three-dimensional works. Carving is the process of subtraction, of ''chipping away,'' as Gross was doing with wood, as Michelangelo had done with marble and Gislebertus with limestone. Modeling is the process of addition, of the accretion of separate quantities of clay or plaster or wax in order to shape a figure or form, as the makers of the Tanagra figurines had done with terra cotta and as sculptors from Andrea Pisano and Ghiberti to Rodin and Lipchitz had done with wax or clay later to be cast in bronze. The two methods are very different, and each has its merits. Questions of vision and taste aside, the purely technical fault of the academic sculpture that dominated the field at the time of Gross's advent was that it attempted to combine the two methods, with the result that all too often the virtues of neither were able to flourish. The successful academic sculptor had the equipment and the studio personnel to operate almost in the style of a mid-twentieth-century designer for mass production. Having produced a small-scale model, in clay or plaster, by the process of addition, he could, and did, have it enlarged mechanically to full size with little personal attention on his part and then, through the employment of a pointing machine, have the full-scale model transferred, as it were, into a block of marble, which, after treatment with machines, would look as if it had somehow been made molten and poured into a mold. It was the equivalent—half a century before younger artists of the mid-twentieth century got around to exploring plastic as a new sculptural medium—of sculpture in plastic.

Furthermore, in his wood carving Gross went beyond the tradition in America and Europe. The wood sculptures of the High Middle Ages, the Renaissance, and the Baroque were almost always worked in soft woods, in many cases fruitwoods, and (like the marble and bronze sculpture of the ancient Greeks) they were made as the ground for painted works of art. They were polychromed or gilded, usually over a layer of gesso. In many instances—especially when the sculpture was intended to stand against a wall and the back was left untreated by gesso and paint— the wood itself rotted away over the centuries, leaving the painted gesso as a shell. In reviving wood as a sculptural medium Gross did not revive the painted surface or the gessoed surface. Nor did he for long stick to the soft woods. As has been said, he found the resistance, the bite, the character of the hard woods responding to something in his own temperament. He thus brought the woods of Africa and South America, of Asia and the South Pacific, into the sculptural tradition of Europe and America.

In dealing with the hard woods—with mahogany, ebony, beefwood, cocobolo, and lignum vitae—Gross from the beginning eschewed the knives and other small-bladed tools of the whittler. This was no hobby he was engaged in: he was not making cuckoo

24

15. MOTHER AND CHILDREN DANCING. 1958. Bronze, height 16″.
Private collection, New York City

clocks or toy soldiers. He was creating form, and he used the classic tools of the sculptor's search for form, the mallet and the chisel—the blade of the chisel turning sensitively in his left hand, now lifted, now low, now angled, now shaving away, now cutting, the weight of the mallet lifted and pounded against the handle of the chisel in an infinite gradation of degrees of force. He has never used power tools, simply because he gets too much sheer physico-aesthetic pleasure out of the process of watching form emerge gradually under his hands.

Very early, Gross found another advantage, an enlargement of the sculptor's vocabulary, in the grain of the hardwoods. A wood sculptor—like a cabinetmaker or a shipwright—has to be keenly aware of the grain of the wood all the time he is working. Normally he works "with the grain," as they say in those trades; when he works against it, he must know why he is doing so and how it will affect the finished work. Out of this intrinsic physical feature of wood Gross has fashioned a means for the enhancement of form. In a way, this deliberate use of the grain is a surface embellishment of the sculptural form related to the polychrome and gilt used by earlier sculptors. But it is in every sense more profound than that, for it comes, after all, out of the material itself: it is essentially a resource of the material. Modern wood carving, as Gross perfected and refined it, takes advantage of the grain not to embellish form, as paint and gilt do, but to reveal it with added force.

When he moved into stone carving Gross brought to bear the habits of eye and hand that he had developed in working in wood. He applied these habits once again when, beginning in the late 1950s, he began turning more and more to bronze as a medium. But he has never given up wood. In the midst of the most ambitious project in bronze, he will still take time to visit the wood studio he maintains on the ground floor of his Greenwich Village house and practice, as it were, on whatever wood piece he happens to have in progress. Significantly, to make the first model for a bronze piece, he customarily works in plaster, not in the soft materials, clay and wax, that so aptly capture the liquid flow of the metal. He builds up the plaster and then carves it away, bringing into play some of the pressure and resistance, the give-and-take of his way with wood. Gross's bronzes retain the look of carved sculpture because the first form has indeed been carved.

Following World War II, American sculpture—and for that matter, contemporary sculpture everywhere—pushed on into new materials and new methods, from found objects to assemblages of various kinds to plastic extrusions and factory-produced minimal boxes, to name a few. Yet Gross's contribution has remained relevant. He had opened the path in this country to the revival of wood and of direct carving at a time when both had been so long in disuse that their appearance constituted a new departure in an art world that was much less enthusiastic about change for its own sake than it has since become.

In addition, Gross has, since he first won recognition in the New Deal days, played a part in the general opening up, freeing, and loosening of conventions that, when he began, were ironclad. It says a good deal that two of his students at the Educational Alliance were Louise Nevelson and, for a short time, Leonard Baskin; the two are worlds apart, and neither is especially close to Gross in the look of the work, but both clearly represent further developments of his interest in wood as a sculptural medium. Wood has since flourished in dozens of hands and in as many styles, and Chaim Gross would be the last to deny the validity of any of them. The names of such diverse sculptors as Raoul Hague, Jennie Lee Knight, Gabriel Kohn, Marisol, Hugh Townley, and H.C. Westermann give a sketchy indication of the highly individual achievements in art and the varied enrichments of the way we can see in art that we owe to Gross.

The New Deal projects enabled Gross to crystallize his own thoughts on sculpture and at the same time to solidify his economic position. When the war effort took precedence over the New Deal, the art projects were speedily phased out, compressed into a war artists' project that, abandoned in turn, was taken over by *Life* magazine. But the projects had brought about a change in America's attitude toward its artists. This was obscured at first because of the overwhelming priorities of World War II; in the midst of the war (December 1942–February 1943), however, the Metropolitan Museum of Art staged a mammoth exhibition of contemporary American art arranged by Artists for Victory, Inc., an emergency wartime association of twenty leading national and New York art societies; of the fourteen purchase prizes awarded by the Museum in sculpture, one of three thousand dollars was won by Chaim Gross. His winning work was an ebony figure of the aerialist Lillian Leitzel, probably the greatest and most glamorous star ever produced by her profession. (The sculptor recalls that it was this sum, which Renee insisted on putting in the bank, that eventually enabled them to buy the house on the Upper West Side where they lived for more than twenty years, until they sold it and bought their house in Greenwich Village, just off Washington Square.) About this time Chaim joined the teaching staff at the Brooklyn Museum Art School, beginning another long-term association. During the New Deal period the Grosses had begun spending their summers teaching in the Berkshires. For a brief time they summered in Rockport, then moved on to join the art community in Provincetown.

All this happened within a dozen years of the time when Chaim was virtually able to eat only by dint of winning nickels at chess. He came in on a new tide of American acceptance of American art, but he does not minimize the part Renee has played in his fortunes since he won that providential fifteen dollars at bingo. "Without a good wife, you're nothing," he once told a reporter for the New York *Post*. "A good wife is half the work done." The sentiment is conventional enough; most men subscribe, or at least give lip service, to this piece of proverbial wisdom. In Gross's case its genuineness derives, on one level, from an extraordinary and effective devotion on the part of Renee, a devotion not only to the person and the work of her husband but also to the details of his artistic career. In connection with his first one-man show, for example, she prevailed upon William Zorach, whom Gross then knew only slightly, to write a few words—while she waited—for the exhibition folder. She has continued this kind of vigorous and valuable auxiliary service ever since, and thus merits acknowledgment for "half the work done." But that tribute—with its submerged and probably subconscious reference to Plato's account of the two halves of the single identity seeking each other and becoming one in the unity of love, which Plato called "the desire and pursuit of the whole"—that tribute tells us more about Chaim Gross than merely that his wife, Renee, has been an immense and invaluable help to him through the years. The briefest visit to the warm, friendly, and hospitable Gross household indicates the nature and the scope of that help.

But the tribute refers also to a basic theme in Gross's work. Although he has carved many single figures (two of the earliest works to gain national attention were the *Alaskan Mail Carrier* for

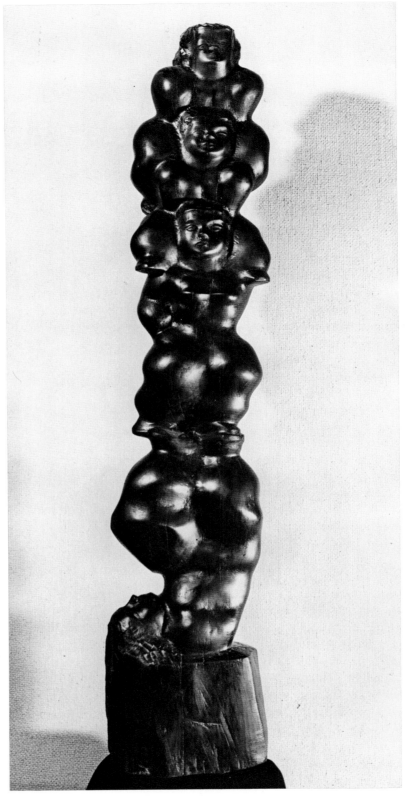

16. FAMILY OF FOUR. 1946. Ebony, height 48″.
Collection Frances Snower, Las Vegas

the Post Office Department and the *Lillian Leitzel* in the Metropolitan Museum of Art), much more dominant in the whole body of his work is the theme of people relating to other people. In the wood sculpture, which often follows the essentially vertical form of the tree that the wood comes from, the relations tend to be vertical. Teams of acrobats, usually two or three, appear one above another; but the real theme, as is amply clear from any detailed examination of these works, is not so much the dexterity or daring of the acrobats as the human quality of the acrobats as symbols of the interdependence of people.

In many of the beautifully carved stone pieces this basic theme takes a different form. Again, the shape is often determined by the material in its original form—a block or a sphere rather than a cylinder as in the case of wood. Within that block or sphere Gross again and again carves a pair of heads or faces so close together, so much part of each other, that at first we cannot entirely follow the line of separation between the one and the other. In the bronzes, to which Gross came relatively late in his career, although he had mastered the essential techniques very early, the theme receives a quite different embodiment: the form is open, space is enclosed rather than merely occupied as in the wood and stone works; implied or actual lines in space, often circular or oval, enclose two or more figures—a mother and child, as in the Jerusalem *Mother Playing,* or a family group, or birds, or children perched like birds on a mother's arm or leg. The vision of two or more human beings as one: this is the great theme of Chaim Gross's sculpture. It is a theme to which he has been faithful, which indeed he has steadily deepened and broadened through the years, always, in one way or another, in disregard of the received doctrine as to the most important task of art. Thus when he began to work, and even more strongly when he was gaining his first, early recognition during the New Deal, there was a powerful urge in American art toward social consciousness, toward sensitivity to the plight of the underprivileged (to use the term then current) and to the manifest injustices of society. That urge—as embodied in the work of such powerful twentieth-century American painters as Levine, Shahn, Evergood—produced many great works of art. Gross, though he clearly shared the social awareness and concern for human values of the people he had grown up with and still associated with, stayed, in his work, all but completely aloof from

17. THE FAMILY. 1963. Bronze, 24 × 31".
Collection Mr. and Mrs. Lewis E. Kern, Woodmere, New York

27

18. SKETCHES FOR SCULPTURE (at left, LILLIAN LEITZEL). 1937. Sepia, 13 1/2 × 18″.
Collection Mimi Gross Grooms, New York City

28

19. The artist at work on VICTORIA. 1951

20. VICTORIA. 1951. Mahogany, height 81″.
Collection Mimi Gross Grooms, New York City

29

this current. Later, perhaps in reaction to that social orientation, it became the received doctrine in the American art world that the artist should concern himself only with his art and with its development, from work to work and within each work. Again Gross disregarded the received doctrine despite its strong appeal for an artist whose joy in his work is perhaps unequaled. It is this immense pleasure he takes in his work and not exaggerated self-esteem that has kept Gross from being swayed by the shifting winds of aesthetic doctrine. He rejected the total preoccupation with the work for its own sake that became fashionable in the 1950s and, in one way or another, has remained so. To the ambitious social involvement of the thirties, Gross opposed his own concern with private persons finding salvation not in social programs but in one another. To the even more ambitious "privatization" of the American artist after World War II he has unfailingly opposed his profound and unfaltering belief in the relation between his art and his humanity.

Gross is a great believer in, and practitioner of, drawing as the mother of the visual arts. It was with drawing that his life as an artist began, back in the Budapest coffeehouses, part of a world long since vanished. He drew constantly when, as a young art student in this country, he assumed that he would become a painter—because that is what he thought all artists were. Since becoming a sculptor he has been drawing consistently, day in and day out—idly, purposefully, from the model, from fantasy, for pleasure, as practical preparation for sculpture. Everything, for Gross, begins in drawing. Besides drawing on paper, he draws on wood and on stone—and then proceeds to follow his drawings into the heart of the wood or the stone, to find there, to liberate, the drawn forms first seen as a blend of the shape of the wood or the stone and the restless, circling movement of his drawing point on paper. From the point of view of Gross's passion for drawing, his eventual move into bronze sculpture after the years in wood and stone was inevitable, even predictable. For bronze, as he handles it, becomes a form of freely moving, three-dimensional drawing in space that it is never possible to achieve in carving stone or wood.

But the carving came first, and wood carving first of all. In one of the earliest pieces by Gross that survives there is a link between the wood sculpture that he was then beginning to awaken from its dormancy and the folk carving that he knew as a child in Galicia.

21 ROOSTER. 1927.
Bronze, height 24 1/2".
Collection Mr. and Mrs. Jack J. Holland,
Lawrence, New York

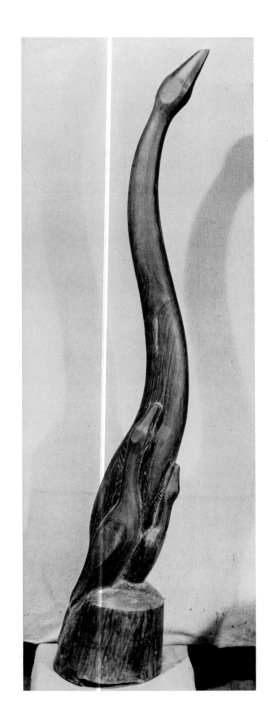

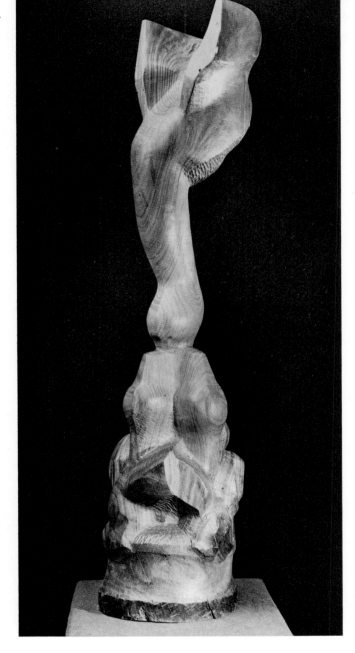

23. BIRD'S NEST. 1940.
Lignum vitae, height 49".
Collection the artist,
New York City

22. MOTHER BIRD. 1951.
Lignum vitae, height 72".
Collection the artist,
New York City

31

24. GIRL IN KIMONO. 1929. Lignum vitae, height 20″.
Collection Mimi Gross Grooms, New York City

25. EAST SIDE GIRL. 1928. Lignum vitae, height 34 3/4″.
Collection Mimi Gross Grooms, New York City

26. TUMBLERS. 1933. Lignum vitae, height 25″.
Collection Bella and Sol Fishko, New York City

27. BLACK FIGURE. 1935. Ebony, height 40″.
Collection Mimi Gross Grooms, New York City

Rooster, which he carved in walnut in 1927, and which he subsequently gave to his son, Yehudah, born in 1935, is much more than just a wonderful divertissement for a child. The elaboration of the tail feathers into a pattern of open arabesques recalls the type of decorative feature seen in folk carving, but Gross went far beyond that in his venture in the revival and extension of the ancient medium. The tail feathers are not single and separate, as they might be in an analogous piece of folk art; they are the grand termination of a motif of swelling arcs and circles that appears in every part of the bird, even the feet. The wings, the leg feathers, the tail feathers (curving down instead of up), the head with its comb, and the breast—all these swell out in pride of being, so that the delightful elaboration of the tail feathers piled up into the air is not so much an added decoration as the logical culmination of the dominant theme.

That Gross's oeuvre includes relatively few animals, whether in wood, stone, or metal, is surprising, considering the felicity with which he has handled such subjects. Two later and spectacularly successful examples are the *Bird's Nest,* of 1940, and the *Mother Bird,* of 1951, both in the hardwood lignum vitae ("wood of life") that has always been a favorite of Gross's. In a way, each work is the reverse of the other, a relation Gross has often used to produce a sequence of pieces on a common theme. The long-necked mother bird almost has to be a goose; yet she is so stylized that the species is not in question—she is bird with young, as is the earlier work. Both give expression to Gross's long-standing preoccupation with mothers and children.

Early works for the government projects reveal other continuing interests. *Helen Tamiris,* the statue of the famous American dancer-choreographer, executed in 1934 for James Monroe High School in the Bronx, shows his masterly skill in making use of the grain of the wood as a means to the delineation of form in the human figure. The two relief-like pieces for the Abraham Lincoln High School, in Brooklyn, executed in mahogany in the same year, reveal an urge toward openwork figure groups, a predilection that Gross was not to realize fully until he moved into bronze on a substantial scale; the same is true of *Puddlers,* the relief he carved in 1940 for the Post Office in Irwin, Pennsylvania.

Fascinated by the remarkable changes in color and tone that take place as the chisel strikes deep into the heart of the hard wood he had begun to use, Gross produced a few figures which exploited that characteristic, but they are not among his best works, even of that early period. He deliberately and somewhat dazzlingly played with color and depth in a few early sculptures of women in evening gowns or furs, the color-depth relation serving to differentiate between flesh and fabric. The opportunity is handled better in *Girl in Kimono,* of 1929, in which the color shift of the lignum vitae suggests differences in texture and also creates a delightful effect in itself, aside from its usefulness as a device.

In those days Gross came as close as he ever did to portraying people in contemporary dress. It is an old problem for the sculptor, one that arose with the Renaissance rediscovery of the Antique, and has never been finally settled. Michelangelo, for instance, put the two dukes in the Medici chapel into the garb of Roman captains, and the reclining figures of that same complex into dateless draperies. Twentieth-century sculptors had no trouble showing Hamilton and Jefferson—to cite two well-known works in our nation's capital—in the dress they actually wore, but sculptors a little closer to their time (Greenough, for example) chose the Roman toga. Even in Gross's *East Side Girl,* one of the better instances of his use of contemporary dress, he seems to be overinfluenced by the spirit of the day, the dictum that the work of the artist should reflect contemporary people and problems. Gross discovered early that his true métier was the human form as such. In part his powerful predilection for circus performers and ballet dancers appears to stem from his realization that both wear costumes that rise above the changing fashions (which somehow date faster in sculpture than in painting) and at the same time reveal or enhance the human form rather than concealing or distorting it.

Before he was thirty, Gross had truly found himself as a sculptor in wood; he had settled on what his search for form would be and even foreseen several of the various routes that that search might take. Stone and bronze were to come later, but the skill in both mediums would flow naturally out of the maturing of the artist in wood.

Tumblers, of 1933, again in lignum vitae, represents an extension of the single figure shaped essentially by the form of the tree trunk. The central part of the double figure, where the two torsos are back to back, almost suggests a huge boll, or knot, in the wood, while the hard grain emphasizes the tension of the limbs and the

28. LEAPFROG. 1931. Lignum vitae, height 17″.
Collection Yehudah Zachary Gross, New York City

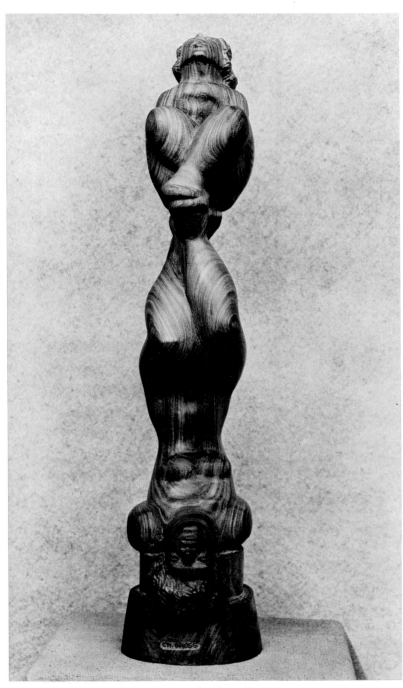

29. BALANCING. 1935. Lignum vitae, height 34″.
Collection Mr. and Mrs. Stanley J. Wolfe, Great Neck, New York

30. MIMI PRAYING. 1947. Lignum vitae, height 33 1/2''.
Collection David A. Teichman, New York City

31. TIGHTROPE DANCER. 1933. Lignum vitae, height 30''.
Collection Mr. and Mrs. John Koehler, Woodmere, New York

spherical shape of the ball balanced on high. This early double figure once more harks back to Plato: the tumblers are two separate parts of the unity created by the expert practice of their skill. The sculptor does not offer, nor do we particularly miss, an absolute line of demarcation between the supporting tumbler and the tumbler balancing the ball on her feet.

Black Figure, of two years later, in ebony, is a remarkable translation of the human body into a rhythmic series of forms. Elbows and knees, often the most intractable parts of the body from the point of view of formal arrangement, are easily and naturally subsumed in an overall shape of great smoothness and flow. The simplification of form arrived at here has been a virtue of Gross's sculpture ever since. Yet, streamlined as it is, *Black Figure* presents an individual human being, not only in the sensitive face but, no less, in the compressed limbs.

Tightrope Dancer, of 1933, demonstrates a magnificent and entirely apposite use of the variations in color of lignum vitae. The change from light to dark faintly suggests some sort of garment, but the effect would never be mistaken for an actual performer's costume. Its more important function is to suggest the flow, over the body, positioned like a ballerina's, of air and motion, of light and of time itself.

Two pieces dating from the early thirties beautifully exemplify Gross's command of the simplification of form: limbs no longer have to serve as limbs; we are happy to accept them fully as further variations on the rounded forms that are the principal components of the female figure. *Leapfrog* and *Balancing,* both in lignum vitae, also take full advantage of that wood's grain. The carving of the figures, with their convexities and concavities, has determined the flow of the grain, which now circles around a knee, a shoulder, or a buttock, now delineates the arch of the chest, now swirls around a thigh or a calf. Even at this early stage of his long adventure with wood, Gross had explored one of its major gifts to the sculptor and had clearly established not only that wood can be as suitable a material for direct carving as stone but also that it has certain peculiar properties of great potential expressiveness.

For Gross the climax of the 1930s was certainly the *Lillian Leitzel,* of 1938. In this figure all the daringly explored and thoroughly mastered technique of using the grain of the wood, in this case macassar ebony, is brought to bear. The grain, more subtle

32. LILLIAN LEITZEL. 1938. Macassar ebony, height 52″.
The Metropolitan Museum of Art, New York City.
Rogers Fund, 1942

33. ACROBATIC PERFORMERS.
1942.
Bronze, height 37″.
Israel Museum,
Jerusalem

34. HEAD TO TOE. 1941. Cuban mahogany, height 34″.
Norton Gallery and School of Art, West Palm Beach, Florida

35. DANCER. 1946. Lignum vitae, height 14 1/4".
Collection Lionel A. Sperber, Q.C., Montreal

36. I LOVE MY BABY. 1948. Lignum vitae, height 53".
The Albert A. List Family Collection, New York City

than that of lignum vitae, washes across the contours of the legs and torso. The arms are not separated but form, with the throat and the upper chest, a continuing surface of rich variety. There is formal balance between the upper part of the figure and the swelling hips, separated by the narrow waist; this duality, which characterizes most of Gross's single figures of the time, echoes the effects he was getting in pairs of figures. Only the flared edge of the skirt suggests the circus performer; for the rest, the sculpture is simply the figure of the performer and, even more, a form found in the wood.

As a wood carver Gross continued to be preoccupied by the circus. This comes through even in small things, like the fact that in the charming 1947 lignum vitae sculpture of his daughter, *Mimi Praying,* there is the same flared skirt edge as is seen in the *Lillian Leitzel.* In rapid succession, glimpses of Gross through the years reveal a veritable procession of circus people: tumblers, rope-dancers, aerialists. From time to time Gross has returned, as in *Acrobatic Performers,* first carved in mahogany in 1942 and then cast in bronze, to the flat relief manner of his early work for the PWAP and the WPA, bringing to it, however, all the sophistication he had acquired in the interval, evidenced in the subtle use of the chisel to create a rhythmic pattern of marks in the skirts and the hair of the two figures. *Head to Toe,* of 1941, is an endless circle of the agile body; in *Dancer,* of 1946, the playful figure stands on her head and shoulders, with legs poised in the air in a position suggesting that perfect balance has not quite been attained in the maneuver.

In *Vanity,* of 1941, Gross turned to a classic medieval and Renaissance theme. The seated girl is regarding herself in a mirror. The hand holding the undelineated mirror is not really free of the solid mass of the block; nor is this, or the other, arm raised over the head to arrange the hair—which, for that matter, is not treated, as Gross sometimes did treat hair, as a separate entity but rather as part of the magnificent flow of the pattern of the grain from top to bottom, even taking in the pedestal on which the figure sits.

The piece is a culmination of the formal discoveries Gross had been making consistently, but it is also—with its intense unity and its elegant graining—an extraordinarily apt embodiment of the subject. His forms have often been compressed and even chunky when considered as actual elements of human bodies, but he has always been capable, when it serves the purposes in hand, of going

40

37. VANITY.
1941.
Lignum vitae, height 30''.
Collection
Mr. and Mrs. Jacob M. Kaplan,
New York City

38. MY SISTER SARAH—IN MEMORIAM. 1947. Vermilion cocobolo, height 68″.
Joseph H. Hirshhorn Foundation, New York City

in the opposite direction of elongation. A superb example of the latter tendency, and a fine treatment of a basic theme, is *I Love My Baby,* with the infant held aloft on the mother's shoulder, almost recalling the acrobats, and the mother's long torso lifting up and out of the swelling hips and legs. The child is a kind of acrobat, joyously feeling the air above with its body and legs, while the mother is, in face and in form, all love, all pride, stretching upward to meet and support the child.

It was inevitable that the members of the Gross family who remained in Galicia would suffer from the second of the great wars even more than they had from the first. *My Sister Sarah—In Memoriam* was carved by Gross in 1947 after he learned that Sarah had perished at the hands of the Nazis. The work, in vermilion cocobolo wood, is a classic Madonna composition. The mother's body leans forward and her face bespeaks total resignation, as if to the cruelty of the world, borne with dignity and therefore with final triumph. Gross's customary economy of form, by means of which separate shapes are indicated but not always actually separated from the main form, serves here to emphasize the oneness of mother and child confronted with overwhelming disaster.

Young Acrobats, of 1952, represents a peak in the expression of Gross's perennial theme of two figures in vertical relation, one supporting the other. The acrobats are not equal: the one above is shorter, and the difference in size almost suggests a mother-child pair. But the ease with which both figures comport themselves reflects accurately the skill of the sculptor in bringing his familiar theme to such a point that we almost accept the two figures as able to exist separately. Their contacts now are more casual than in any earlier such piece. The upper figure is poised as if on air, in the manner of Dürer's *Nemesis (The Large Fortune)* balancing in the wind. The pattern of the lignum vitae grain appears at its loveliest, unifying the figures and whispering of lights and breezes. The acrobats are in dynamic control of themselves and their muscles, yet there is no sense of strain, or even of intense concentration. They work as they exist, the product of habit so cultivated as to become, like the wood, part of their being.

Other themes augment the group that includes this vertical pair. *Dancing Mother,* of 1954, carved in mahogany in a manner that preserves something of the early stage of blocking out the figure yet combines it with the final stage of smooth finish, deals with a theme

40. ROCK-A-BYE. 1954. Walnut, length 14″.
The Kimmel Family Collection, New York City

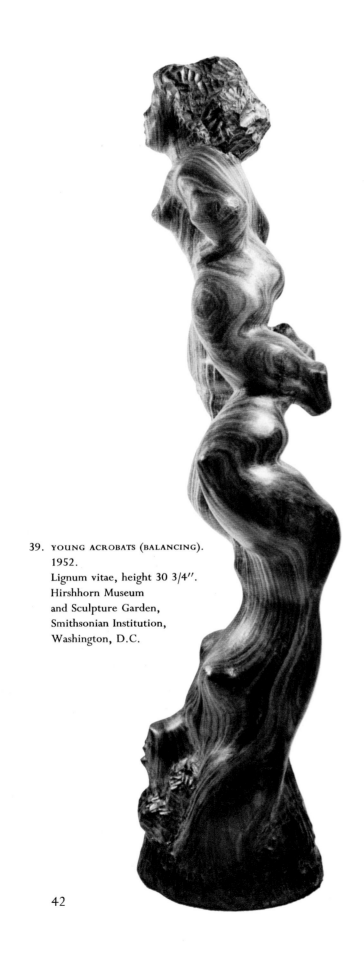

39. YOUNG ACROBATS (BALANCING).
1952.
Lignum vitae, height 30 3/4″.
Hirshhorn Museum
and Sculpture Garden,
Smithsonian Institution,
Washington, D.C.

41. Albrecht Dürer. NEMESIS (THE LARGE FORTUNE).
c. 1501–3. Engraving

42

42. PROUD MOTHER.
1954.
Ebony, 30 × 11″.
Forum Gallery,
New York City

43. DANCING MOTHER. 1954. Mahogany, height 17″.
Collection Renee Nechin Gross, New York City

that Gross subsequently pursued in depth in bronze. So does *Rock-a-Bye,* of 1954, in walnut, which at the same time continues a Gross mutation of the vertical into the horizontal.

Perhaps the most complete departure from the traditional, and all but inescapable, verticality of a form of art that in large part has to depend upon the cylinder of the tree trunk is found in two pieces of the period, the ebony *Mother and Child,* of 1954, and the mahogany *Sisters,* of two years later. The latter, a double piece, is most unusual in Gross's work, the two forms appearing side by side rather than one above the other in conformity with the natural growth pattern of wood. The lustrous finish, the fine, close grain, and the expert utilization of the happy flaw—the line that crosses the torso of the sister on the right diagonally—all these contribute to the impression that the figures are emerging from the wood even as we watch; the surface of the wood appears almost as a transparent veil over the two girls, recalling to mind the veiled faces of, say, Medardo Rosso. This work represents, too, a climactic point in the total control of the medium—or rather the total union of the medium and the methods—that Gross has acquired, or grown into, in his decades as the leading sculptor in wood in America. The ebony piece also breaks away from the single-cylinder form; the child on the mother's shoulder is as substantial as the mother herself, so that the work presents a formal duality different in kind and in implication from the linear, or serial, duality (or multiplicity) of most of his earlier sculptures. The two works, together, anticipate the theme of union, or two-in-one, pursued in his other mediums, stone and bronze.

It is not surprising that Gross continued in stone, to a certain extent, what he had perfected in wood. The process of creation was very similar—that "chipping away" toward a form perceived in drawings and in the study of the original block. The *Sisters* of 1946, carved in pink Italian marble, is right out of the circus repertory and could have been carved in wood. Almost two decades later, *Vanity* of 1962, in serpentine stone, renews a theme earlier expressed in wood but shows the figure even more compact, still deriving strength from the daring amalgamation of individual limbs into swelling body masses. Some highly original female pairs of the early 1940s—two versions of *Rock-a-Bye* and one *Eternal Mother,* all in lithium stone—elaborate the duality Gross was reaching for in wood. The two *Rock-a-Bye*'s also exemplify Gross's ability to give a

44. SISTERS. 1956. Mahogany, height 28".
Collection Mr. and Mrs. Lewis Garlick, New York City

45. SISTERS. 1946. Italian pink marble, height 41".
Whitney Museum of American Art, New York City

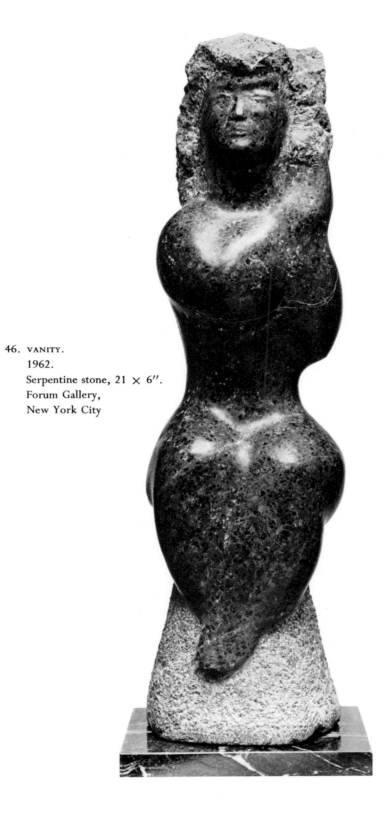

46. VANITY.
1962.
Serpentine stone, 21 × 6".
Forum Gallery,
New York City

47. ROCK-A-BYE. 1941. Lithium stone, length 25″.
Collection Mr. and Mrs. Saul Rosen, Paterson, New Jersey

48. ROCK-A-BYE. 1943. Lithium stone, length 18″.
Whereabouts unknown

specific form to a theme and then, by changing only one element, to turn it into something altogether different. In the case of these two sculptures it is the degree of finish applied to the stone that works the transformation. Though the form of the two works is almost identical, the 1941 piece is softer, more matte, more open as compared to the 1943 piece, which is rich and full of lights.

But while much was carried over from one medium to the other, the sculptor also learned to let the forms inherent in the stone survive into the finished work in a way different from the way the forms inherent in the wood survive. A series of pieces in white and in pink alabaster convey the impression that the forms are on the point of emerging from clouds of the milky stone. At first glance *In the Sun,* of 1947, could be mistaken for a cloud mass. Even after the face and the legs are distinguished, the cloud image coexists with that of the swelling, floating figure. Gross used this soft, yielding medium again for a figure he added to the group of the Seven Deadly Sins he had begun with *Vanity. Lust,* of 1955, poses the figure upside down, the head at the bottom of a profusion of soft white flesh swelling up into the air. Doubtless many a medieval sermon was based on the concept of lust confounding man's reason and expanding into disproportion his weak flesh; the sculptor's focus is rather on the helplessness of the victim and, as always, on the beauty of the volumes and surfaces of the form.

Alabaster provided the medium also for a remarkable series of sculptures of the early 1950s expressing the theme of duality that, as we have seen, permeates Gross's work—twins, lovers, sisters, mothers and children. In *Embrace,* of 1951, in pink alabaster, the bodies of the lovers melt into one and dissolve into a graceful swag of cloud, their faces emerging from and borne by its lightness—an unexpected and felicitous adaptation of the Renaissance and Baroque device of the cloud of cherubim and seraphim afloat in the sky. The theme is varied in the *Twins,* of 1953, in which the two faces seem to come together in an aerial maneuver, as if hovering over the unseen earth in a mood of concerned bliss. *The Pink Cloud,* of the following year, carries the unity in duality theme one logical but bold step further: the two faces are conceived as having begun to blend into each other. They look straight out at us from the cloud of limbs and torsos fused into a shapely mass, and we gradually realize that there are only three eyes. Perhaps because of Gross's early predilection for hard wood, the most completely successful

46

50. IN THE SUN. 1947. White alabaster, height 9 1/2".
Whereabouts unknown

49. LUST. 1955. White alabaster, height 14".
Collection Harriet Romain Weiss, New York City

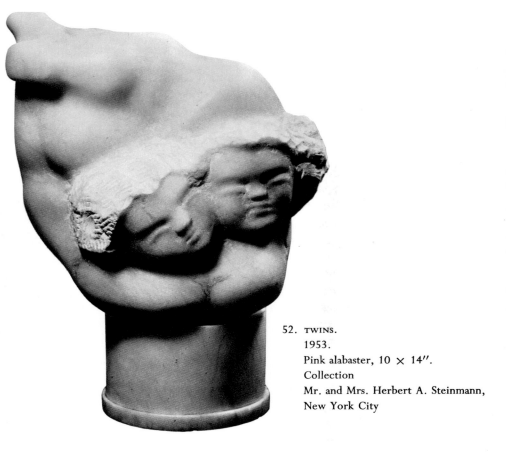

52. TWINS.
1953.
Pink alabaster, 10 × 14″.
Collection
Mr. and Mrs. Herbert A. Steinmann,
New York City

51. EMBRACE.
1951.
Pink alabaster, length 15″.
Collection Mr. and Mrs. Jacob D. Weintraub, New York City

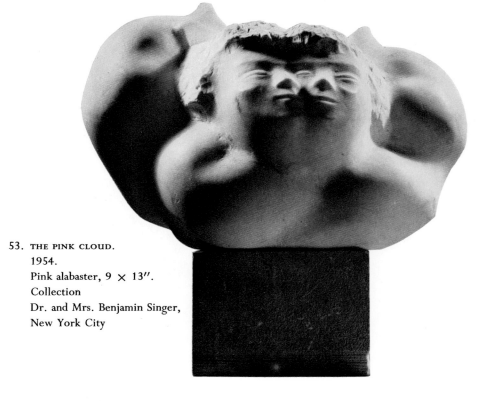

53. THE PINK CLOUD.
1954.
Pink alabaster, 9 × 13″.
Collection
Dr. and Mrs. Benjamin Singer,
New York City

example in this series is *Little Sisters,* of 1954, in serpentine, a harder stone. The masterly exploitation of the stone's grain enhances the soaring form and gives it a new continuity. Familiar points and planes of anatomy can be discerned within the stone; at the same time, the stone is not a machine for soaring—as were the early acrobats in wood with their tensed and dynamic muscles—but shaped atmosphere, as it were, the spirit of soaring, set free from the earth's gravity, afloat in the sustaining medium of love, in the lofty mode of unity.

In general, Gross approaches portraiture with some reluctance; indeed he has for the most part avoided it. In personal expression he has always found the human figure more in accord with his vision than the human face. More often than not, both in his wood and in his bronze works, the face serves as a focal point for the body or for the relation between two or more bodies. However, Gross has not altogether eschewed a form that has been a staple of the sculptor's art, going back at least as far as ancient Mesopotamia and Egypt and marked by such high points as the Greco-Roman portrait heads, the busts of Bernini and Houdon, the small sculptured heads of Daumier, the portrait heads of Jacob Epstein. For whatever reason, Gross has carved only a very few portrait heads in wood—his own, his wife's, his son's, and one or two others—whereas in stone he has executed a whole series of powerful examples. These heads in stone are not portraits in the strictest sense: while not idealizations, like his figures of Pride, Vanity, and Lust, they are essays in the human physiognomy, undertaken in much the same spirit as his essays in the human form. In these heads, as in the wood aerialists and tumblers, human and formal values meet, fuse, and enhance one another. The series begins with *Roxanne,* carved in lithium in 1940. The head is raised as if to the sun, eyes closed, the planes of the face enlarged and elaborated in the planes of the hair, which is treated abstractly as a richly profuse mass of chisel marks, not polished and rubbed into smoothness like the face. *Head of Anne,* of the following year, carved in Belgian black marble, is completely different, an authentic evocation of a twentieth-century urban face, at the same time recalling, in its formal balancing of masses, above and below, and in its frank use of the stonecutter's points for surface effect, more primitive carvings, those of Africa, Haiti, or Easter Island. *Lucretia,* also of 1941, in lithium, allows what appears to be the untouched, raw

54. LITTLE SISTERS. 1954. Serpentine stone, height 14″.
Collection the artist, New York City

49

56. HEAD OF ANNE.
1941.
Belgian black marble,
height 8 1/2".
Forum Gallery,
New York City

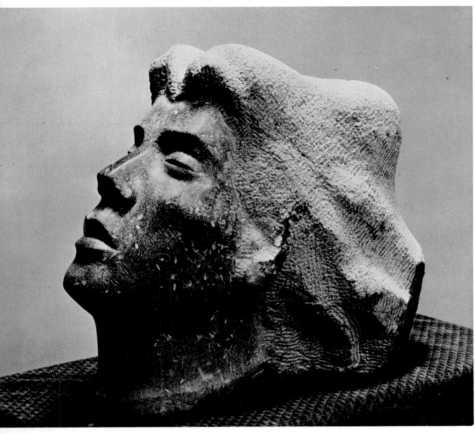

55. ROXANNE.
1940.
Lithium stone, height 14".
Collection
Mr. and Mrs. Saul Rosen,
Paterson, New Jersey

57. LUCRETIA.
1941.
Lithium stone,
height 12 1/2".
Joseph H. Hirshhorn Foundation,
New York City

58. ZIPORAH. 1954. Serpentine stone, height 9″.
Collection Mr. and Mrs. Jan Peerce, New Rochelle, New York

stone to serve as the massive coiffure, so that the face seems to emerge from the virgin rock, glinting with its veins and lights, like a pure product of nature. Something of the same effect is attained in *Ziporah,* of 1954, in serpentine stone. Both works are enhanced by the polishing that gives the face form and texture, and, in an equal and opposite way, by the connection with the bedrock, which also serves to suggest a mass of hair.

The duality of so much of the wood sculpture and of the "cloud" figures in alabaster also appears in the stone heads, in particularly beautiful, ingenious, and moving embodiments. *Reflection,* of 1957, in rich serpentine, states the theme clearly, the face above being reversed in the face below, the two joined not only by the shared throat but by the hair masses and, most tellingly, by the line down the cheek. A true Chaim Gross invention, the work arouses wonder that no sculptor thought of it earlier, for the idea, once seen, seems so logical as to be inevitable. Yet, so far as a reasonably thorough search can establish, the one previous analogy in art to Gross's dual heads emerging from clouds of stone occurs in the Correggio painting *Jupiter and Io,* where the god materializes in the cloud embraced by the maiden. In the dark, planed surfaces of the *Naomi and Ruth* of 1956 the Old Testament story of the two women who cleave to each other is eloquently told. It is significant that Gross came back to the scriptural tale and to the same basic form almost ten years later, once more in lithium stone but with a slight change of emphasis, so that the upper face is clearly supporting the lower, giving dedicated strength in the common ordeal.

In bronze, Gross has executed a number of superb portrait heads. Among his subjects are the Yiddish poet Nochum Yud; Chaim Weizmann, Israel's first president, and his wife, Vera; Gross's daughter, Mimi; his fellow artists Karl Knaths and Moses Soyer; and the guitarist Andrés Segovia. An outstanding portrait is that of the artist's friend Harold Ruttenberg, writer, industrialist, and supporter of the arts in America and Israel.

There are works in bronze by Gross dating from 1940 and earlier, but bronze did not really become his medium until after 1950. In the fifties, sixties, and seventies, he moved at last without reservation into this great classic medium of the sculptor. Sculpture in bronze is an additive art, sculpture in stone and wood, subtractive. Yet, it bears repeating, the way of Gross in bronze has

59. REFLECTION. 1957. Serpentine stone, height 13″.
Collection Mr. and Mrs. Lawrence Richmond, Great Neck, New York

60. NAOMI AND RUTH. 1956. Lithium stone, height 26″.
Collection Renee Nechin Gross, New York City

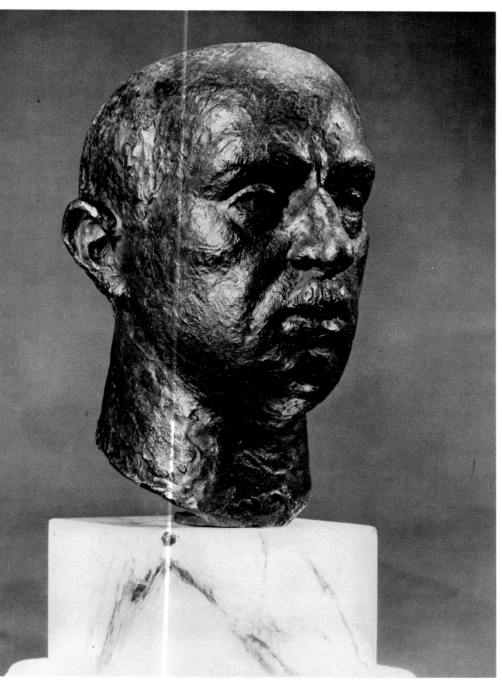

61. NOCHUM YUD. 1924. Bronze, life size.
Private collection, Worcester, Massachusetts

not at all been the opposite of his way in stone and wood. On the contrary, the later medium has profited immensely from his years with the two earlier ones. For the sculptor in bronze, all things are possible. There are very few limitations, and those few can usually be gotten around by the thoughtful application of ingenuity derived from experience. The wood sculptor begins with a tree trunk: whatever he wants to do has to be done within that narrow cylinder. The stone sculptor begins with a block of stone: whatever he wants to do has to be done within that block. In total contrast, the sculptor in bronze begins with his idea, his vision. The clay or wax or (as in Gross's case) the plaster will accommodate itself to whatever he sees in his mind. It will stretch, it will open up, it will enclose space—and so will the bronze that is cast in its image. The freedom of the bronze sculptor is, of course, a magnificent opportunity, as artists have realized from the early days of civilization, but it is also a danger, as has been realized by such great sculptors as Michelangelo, whose bronzes were few and far between. Gross must be considered fortunate in the extreme for having come to bronze only after years, not of apprenticeship but of mastership in the older, more difficult, more circumscribed mediums of stone and wood. The sheer discipline of direct carving is part of his advantage, but more than that is involved. His bronzes contain—or, more accurately, are contained by—the limitations, the difficulty of the carving method. Like any modeling sculptor, Gross builds his form up from nothing by the slow, steady accretion of substance onto the armature, but he also, like any carving sculptor, creates his form out of an existing space, density, texture, weight, all of which happen to be invisible to the eye, intangible to the hand, yet ultimately are present to the total sense perception of the viewer.

An understanding of the difference between the two methods—carving and modeling—is essential to a full appreciation of what Gross has achieved in his bronzes. The difference is probably most easily grasped through historical comparison. Michelangelo is said to have made the observation that a sculpture is good when it can be rolled down a hill without any of its parts breaking off. This is an exaggeration, of course, but the ideal thus expressed is the ideal of carved sculpture. The criterion is met by the great Florentine's *Pietà*, by his *David*, by the recumbent figures in the Medici tombs. It is also met by the majority of Chaim Gross's

62. The artist at work on his bust of Karl Knaths. 1966

sculptures in wood and stone. The *Naomi and Ruth* of 1956, for example, would outroll most of Michelangelo's marble statues on the hills of Tuscany; it is an astonishing realization of Michelangelo's ideal for sculpture: a solid block of stone which miraculously reveals the two heads, the spirits, the sensitive, questing souls, of the two women without losing anything of the sheer block quality of the stone.

So much for carving. How different is bronze, with its modeling and casting. If the modeler can get his mock-up to hold together until its hollow interior is filled with anima and its exterior form is surrounded with a mold, the cast bronze will take whatever shape he has envisaged. The only boundaries are those of the sculptor's imagination; there is no block, no trunk of wood.

Appreciating the difference between the two mediums aids our perception of the greatness of the achievement of Chaim Gross in bronze, for in Gross's work we see combined the contrasting talents that the two materials demand. The combination, moreover, embodies a vision of Gross's that has been implicit in his work since the earliest days of "chipping away." Although Gross will undoubtedly be remembered in art history as the sculptor who was largely responsible for reviving wood as a medium, his most complex achievement is, surprisingly, in bronze—the product of his disciplined years of direct carving, modulated into the freedom of bronze without loss of the tightness of carving.

Gross's mature synthesis of the carving discipline and the casting freedom is an artistic paradox, readily demonstrated by almost any of the bronzes from, say, 1950 on. It is true enough—and neither surprising nor unexpected—that his bronze works contain numerous echoes of his carving in wood or stone: some bronzes, indeed, are straight translations of the carved forms. It was bronze that lured Gross into portraiture even though he was not really attracted to that genre, and his portrait heads in this medium carry on the sculptor's sensitivity as demonstrated in wood and stone. Likewise, the circus piece *Tumbler*, in bronze, is a small work that essentially repeats and refines forms that Gross had already discovered and delineated in wood and stone. The shimmer of light on the bronze lends a new reality, a new aura of perception, to the piece, which is in fact virtually unchanged; it is still, as it was, one of the perfect shapes. *Balancing* of 1935, in highly polished bronze, was directly cast from the carved lignum vitae *Balancing* of

63. TUMBLER. 1966. Bronze, 11 × 9″. Private collection, Detroit

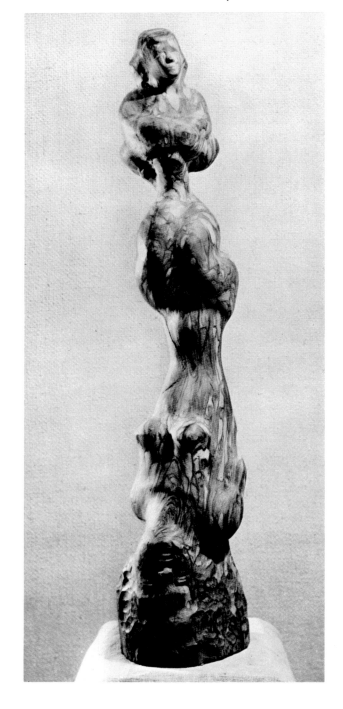

64. BABY BALANCING. 1950. Cocobolo wood, height 29 1/2".
Collection the artist, New York City

65. BALANCING (detail)

66. BALANCING. 1935. Bronze, 35 × 7 × 9″.
Whitney Museum of American Art, New York City.
Gift of Chaim and Renee Gross

the same year. But both these works, and indeed many of Gross's tightly composed, even compressed, forms in wood, such as the *Baby Balancing* of 1950, reveal, in that compression, the essential form that has, in expansion, shaped most of his work in bronze.

That form, as has been said, is the sphere—and its section, the circle. The shapes that enchant us in the vertical "Balancing" pieces are the series of spheres emerging from the towers of acrobatic muscle. Knees and shoulders are knobby, bony projections of the human anatomy, and so they have been for most sculptors of the human figure. Gross has consistently, in his carved work, amalgamated them into spheres, so that, in these vertical compositions, the knees and shoulders join with the breasts and buttocks, stomachs and heads, to form a falling rhythm of spheres, a cascading solar system in miniature. These contained spheres and circles of the carved work are set free and enlarged in the bronzes. Very often the sphere is made quite explicit: the figures are enclosed in circles or hold aloft circles that contain other, small figures—children or birds. More typically, perhaps, the circles are implied rather than stated: the figures form substantial parts of a circle, or their motions imply a great circle in which they move, or a mother playing with her children forms, with her own torso and limbs, the section of a sphere that, if it were actual, would enclose and protect the children in a self-sufficient little world of their own (the Jerusalem *Mother Playing* is a case in point). The schematic analysis of Renaissance paintings by such scholars as Wölfflin and Berenson often included diagrams of the movement in the works with curving arrows crossing or meeting. If the bronze sculptures of Chaim Gross were so analyzed, a great many pieces, probably most of the substantial ones, would be found to project an enclosing sphere as his most typical form, or a circle as his most characteristic movement.

The openness of bronze has afforded Gross the opportunity to execute some religious projects. On the whole, the religious theme is rare in his work, and this is odd: although, like many artists, somewhere in the transition between adolescence and young manhood he left his traditional, family religion behind, Gross, unlike many, returned to the faith of his fathers. He has never had any desire to revisit the Galicia of his childhood, since the world he knew and loved there was destroyed in World War II, but visiting Israel, which came into existence partly as the aftermath

57

of that war, Gross has felt, despite the enormous differences of climate and atmosphere, that he was returning to his homeland. The experience effectively brought him back to Judaism, and he is a reverent visitor to, among other synagogues, a Hasidic congregation in the Williamsburg section of New York City. As an expression of this renewal of religious feeling, Gross has produced an impressive series of eight-branched menorahs, or Hanukkah lamps (the terms are used interchangeably in the titles of the works). Hanukkah, the Festival of Lights, celebrates the victory of the Maccabees over the Syrians. The festival lasts for eight days; starting with a single light, each evening one more candle on the ritual candelabrum is lighted. Since the establishment of the State of Israel, Hanukkah has taken on deepened significance for Jews; a less historic reason for the importance of the holiday in America especially has been its chronological closeness to Christmas. This coincidence Gross has simply taken up into his art by creating, in several instances, menorahs in the shape of trees, with trunks and branches, sometimes sheltering birds and sometimes bearing lights—a conception that in fact carries on an age-old Middle Eastern tradition linking the menorah and the tree of life. At the same time it constitutes a gesture of Judeo-Christian unity in line with and even somewhat ahead of the conversations and exchanges of thought that the two faiths have been engaging in during the last several decades. But Gross's lamps all have in common the creative vision of the artist responding to the mystical meanings within a ceremonial object, meanings to which its users are not always sensitive. In the dancing figures, in the lift of birds, the very spirit of liberation from bondage is evoked. With no loss to the basic liturgical function of the lamp it is illumined by a new light, the light of the human spirit exploring its religious heritage.

When the nature of Hasidic Judaism is understood, it becomes clear that the menorahs are far from being Chaim Gross's only religious works. Hasidic Jews sing and dance in celebration of the Sabbath and festivals and in general honor the admonition of the Baal Shem Tov, the teacher and religious leader who founded this movement, in the eighteenth century, that one must serve God in joy. They are the Jews so memorably painted by Max Weber; it is their lifting, buoyant spirit that animates the village, or *shtetl*, in Chagall's pictures of life in old Russia. In terms of otherworldly religions, the spirit of the Hasidim may be compared with the in-

67. MENORAH WITH BIRDS.
1963.
Welded metal (unique),
78 × 48″.
Collection the artist,
New York City

nocent spirit of the original Franciscan friars before the elaborate institutionalization of the order, or to Zen Buddhism, with its joyous drive to bring man's mind back to the simplest truths of human experience. The spirit that informs most of Gross's sculpture is akin to these spiritual currents with their disposition toward rejoicing in the gifts of life and love, and in this sense his works are indeed religious.

Early in his career Gross remarked to a critic that he loved making his acrobats and would make as many as he could because he so enjoyed being with them. The acrobats have gradually revealed themselves as representing the human family, especially mothers with their children. It requires no particularly profound analysis to trace the origin of that theme's significance for Chaim Gross: it relates, as has been suggested, to his childhood memories of family life in Galicia and its shattering in World War I and to his joy in the motherhood of Renee and in their two children.

The circus, offering us a heightened image of ourselves in the entire gamut of ambition, achievement, and self-mockery, has been a favorite theme of many artists. The melancholy clown comes down to us from Watteau, and we know him from his haunting embodiments in the work of Rouault and the early Picasso. The circus itself, as an entity, has been presented as a microcosm of humanity by such diverse creative artists as Ruggiero Leoncavallo, in *Pagliacci,* Philip Barry, in *Here Come the Clowns,* Leonid Andreyev, in *He Who Gets Slapped.* Chaim Gross's vision of the circus has both widened and deepened since his early essays into the theme, among them the prize-winning sculpture of *Lillian Leitzel.* The acrobats in carved wood have gradually been replaced or augmented by family themes, yet the change has taken place with no loss at all of the atmosphere of the circus, especially of the virtuosos of beauty in balance. Mother and child appear as if performers in routines requiring great skill, long practice, absolute trust in each other. They are happy in each other, the sculptor seems to be telling us, and their happiness is the sustaining bond that keeps the miraculous balance—defying gravity, evading collapse, surviving in joyous triumph. The endless circles that the familial performers hold up, or that they form with their own bodies, echo, of course,

the circles of the rings wherein the circus skills are displayed, as well as the great globe itself on which we all live out our lives.

It is true that the family as miniature circus troupe appears in Gross's work more often than not without the husband-father. It is mothers and children who play with each other, the happy mother leaning back and lifting her children like birds poised for flight or sitting and holding them like the miniature adults that Early Renaissance painters placed alongside the normal-sized saints. Yet the father-husband is far from absent: it is his eyes that take in the vision of mother and children at play—and his hands that have fashioned the vision into bronze. All artists are present in their work in one way or another, whether explicitly, as in the anxious self-portrait of Tiepolo in one corner of the breathtakingly aerial ceiling in the Würzburg Residenz and in the witty works with which Picasso enlivened his old age (Portraits of the Artist as a Dirty Old Man, as it were), or implicitly, as in many of Renoir's paintings, where the viewer senses the presence of the artist through the enormous pleasure he takes in the vision he is presenting, a pleasure so intense that it becomes part of the work. This is not a quality that can be easily isolated in Gross, any more than it can in Renoir, but it is sensed in work after work. We feel the pleasure of the sculptor in the vision of these lifting, soaring, delicately balanced forms. That the figures themselves relish what they are doing is obvious, but their pleasure is in part a reflection of the delight the artist takes in capturing the particular fraction of reality that they represent and successfully translating it into art.

Chaim Gross has given us solid sculptural form in an age when that classic value is being rediscovered and explored anew. In an age which has seen many sculptors reaching out for new materials and new methods, Chaim Gross has made a significant and enduring contribution to the rediscovery of an ancient medium, wood, and the equally ancient methods of shaping it. But beyond the achievement that gives him a secure place in the history of art in our time, he has, in his work, again and again given us joy, the most precious gift the artist can offer the human community of which he is part. He has celebrated with happiness and love the sacrament of life— his chosen theme.

68. The artist at work on BALANCING. 1968

BIOGRAPHICAL OUTLINE

1904   Born March 17, in Galician village of Wolowa, East Austria, tenth child of Moses Gross, lumber merchant, and wife, Leah (Sperber).

1911   Family moves to Kolomyya, where better schooling is available.

1914   During the first weeks of World War I, Kolomyya is scene of pillage and destruction; possession of the town passes back and forth between the invading Russians and the Austrians and a period of upheaval, homelessness, and deprivation begins for the Grosses and thousands of other war refugees.

1916–18   Family flees from Russian reign of terror, joining Jewish exodus from Kolomyya; Chaim is separated from his parents but is finally reunited with them in Austrian Silesia.

1919   Makes his way to Vienna, with his brother Abraham, searching for their eldest brother, Pincus, who is finally found in Budapest. In Budapest, begins drawing in spare time while supporting himself with odd jobs and apprentice gold- and silversmith work; enters a competition and wins a full scholarship to art school, his first formal contact with art. Under the reactionary Horthy regime is imprisoned, along with Abraham, and then deported to Austria. Back in Vienna with Abraham, subsists on odd jobs, but is able to attend the Kunstgewerbeschule.

1921   On April 14 reaches New York with Abraham; finds brother Naftoli, who has helped them immigrate, on the East Side. Starts work as delivery boy. Attends the Educational Alliance Art School, where he makes friends with Moses and Raphael Soyer, Peter Blume, and Adolph Gottlieb and gets to know Ben Shahn and Barnett Newman.

1925   Continuing at the Educational Alliance Art School, attends classes also at the Beaux-Arts Institute of Design, where Elie Nadelman is his teacher.

1927   Decides to concentrate on sculpture; quits his job and his classes at the Educational Alliance Art School and the Beaux-Arts Institute of Design but enrolls at the Art Students League for a short period of instruction, under Robert Laurent, in direct-carving techniques. Rents a room on East Fourteenth Street and devotes all his time to sculpture. Lives from hand to mouth, at one point working briefly in a machine embroidery shop, at another taking a dishwashing job, but achieves his first earnings through art —by the sale of works and by teaching at the Educational Alliance Art School.

1930   By this year has carved figures in forty different types of wood (now in collections throughout the United States).

1932   First one-man exhibition (sculpture and drawings), Gallery 144 West 13th Street, New York (March 5–25). Marries Renee Nechin, December 13.

1933   Awarded Louis Comfort Tiffany Foundation Fellowship. In addition to carving wood sculptures, models many figures of athletes, dancers, etc., in plaster.

1934   Teaches wood carving during the summer months at Playhouse in the Hills, Cummington, Massachusetts (also in 1935, 1936).

69. The artist with THE LINDBERGHS AND HAUPTMANN. 1932

1935   One-man exhibition, Boyer Galleries, Philadelphia. Joint exhibition with Ahron Ben-Shmuel, Guild Art Gallery, New York. Son, Yehudah M. Zachary (Yudie), born July 10.

1936   Wins commission (one of twelve) from the Section of Painting and Sculpture, U.S. Treasury Department, in national competition for art work for public buildings; *Alaskan Mail Carrier,* in cast aluminum, receives $3,000 prize.

1937   Awarded silver medal (second prize) of the Exposition Universelle, Paris, for sculpture *Offspring.* One-man exhibition (sculptures and drawings), Boyer Galleries, New York (February 8–27). *Handlebar Riders* acquired by Museum of Modern Art, New York.

1938   Wins second commission from Section of Fine Arts, U.S. Treasury Department, to execute a sculpture (*Riveters*) for the doorway of the Federal Trade Commission Building in Washington, D.C. Represented in first Municipal Art Exhibition sponsored by Mayor Fiorello La Guardia in the Forum of the RCA Building in Rockefeller Center, New York. Carving of *Head of Renee* in sabicu wood is recorded in three-reel 16 mm. film, "Tree Trunk to Head," directed by Lewis Jacobs, photographed by Leo Lances, produced by Film Associates. Begins two-year period of teaching wood and stone carving at the Design Laboratory, New York.

1939   Executes plaster relief *Harvest,* for the France Overseas building, and *Linesman,* for the Finland building of the New York World's Fair. One-man exhibition, Cooperative Gallery, Newark (May 10–June 1). Represented in Sculptors' Guild outdoor exhibition, New York.

1940   Creates *Ballerina* in the sculpture demonstration

70. The artist's studio. 1941. Foreground: NOVICE (on loan to Tel Aviv Museum, Israel)

series arranged by the New York City WPA Art Project at the American Art Today pavilion at the World's Fair, working for two months "before 160,000 eyes." Receives commission from the U.S. Treasury Department, Section of Fine Arts, for sculptured relief for the Post Office of Irwin, Pennsylvania. Represented (*Lillian Leitzel; Circus Girl*) in "Exhibition of Paintings and Sculpture by the Art School Alumni of the Educational Alliance" (October 7–22), commemorating the twenty-fifth anniversary of the founding of the Educational Alliance Art School, New York. Daughter, Miriam (Mimi), born September 25.

1941   Three works—*Self-Portrait, Acrobatic Dance,* and *Circus Girls*—shown in traveling exhibition of sculpture in wood circulated by American Federation of Arts to university and college museums. *Girl on Wheel* purchased by the Metropolitan Museum of Art, New York.

1942   *Lillian Leitzel,* shown in Artists for Victory exhibition, Metropolitan Museum of Art, New York (December 7–February 22, 1943), wins $3,000 purchase prize. One-man exhibition (sculptures, watercolors, and drawings), Associated American Artists Galleries, New York. Begins teaching at Brooklyn Museum Art School. *Acrobatic Dancers* purchased by Whitney Museum of American Art, New York.

1943   Teaches at Museum of Modern Art Peoples Art Center (where he continues to teach for six years). Named to Educational Alliance Hall of Fame on the occasion of its fiftieth anniversary.

1946   One-man show (watercolors and drawings), Associated American Artists Galleries, New York (January 21–February 7).

1947   One-man exhibition (sculptures and drawings), Associated American Artists Galleries, New York (October 6–25).

1948   One-man exhibition, Associated American Artists Galleries, New York. Joins art faculty of the New School for Social Research, New York.

1949   Sketch for (unrealized) sculpture monument *In Memoriam to Six Million Jews of Europe* exhibited, along with sketches by the five other finalists in the competition, in the Jewish Museum, New York. Published: *Chaim Gross, Sculptor,* by Josef Vincent Lombardo. Makes first trip to Israel; as one of eleven American artists instrumental in collecting a gift to the State of Israel of over 140 paintings by American artists, attends open-

71. The artist at work carving EASTER SUNDAY. 1948

ing exhibition of these works at the Tel Aviv Art Museum. Travel: from Israel, journeys to Paris, Istanbul, and Switzerland.

1950   Teaches at Five Towns Music and Art Foundation, Woodmere, New York.

1951   Traveling exhibition of over thirty life-size photographs of Gross executing a sculpture in wood, organized by the Museum of Modern Art, New York, through its education program, begins two-year circuit through college and university museums. One-man exhibition (sculptures and drawings), Philadelphia Art Alliance. Awarded first prize for watercolor, Cape Cod Art Association, Hyannis, Massachusetts. Travel: spends three months in Israel, painting forty privately commissioned watercolors; also visits Italy, Amsterdam, Rotterdam, Paris, London.

1952   One-man exhibitions: "Chaim Gross: Fantastic Watercolors and Drawings," Associated American Artists Galleries, New York (January 7–26); sculptures and drawings, State Teachers College, New Paltz, New York (February 3–24).

1953   Honored by testimonial dinner sponsored by the Palette Club, student organization of the Educational Alliance Art School, to mark his twenty-fifth year of teaching at the school. Forty watercolors painted in Israel in 1951 exhibited (with twenty-five sculptures, the earliest dating from 1931) at the Jewish Museum, New York (May–July).

1954   Wins honorable mention in sculpture for *I Love My Baby,* shown in 149th Annual Exhibition of Painting and Sculpture, Pennsylvania Academy of the Fine Arts, Philadelphia. *Black Figure* awarded third prize for sculpture, Boston Arts Festival. *Chaim Weizmann* (bronze portrait bust) acquired by Municipal Museum of Modern Art, Haifa. One-man exhibition (sculptures, watercolors, drawings), Shore Studio Gallery, Boston. Represented in American Jewish Tercentenary contemporary fine arts exhibit, shown in New York (Riverside Museum) and a number of other cities, including Philadelphia (Art Alliance), Rochester, New York (Memorial Art Gallery, The University of Rochester), Chicago, Dallas (Museum of Fine Arts), Buffalo (Albright-Knox Art Gallery), Washington, D.C. (Corcoran Gallery of Art).

1955   *Deborah,* shown in 13th Annual Exhibition of Audubon Artists, Inc., New York, awarded Anonymous Prize for Sculpture.

1956   Receives annual Arts and Letters Award of $1,000 from the National Institute of Arts and Letters, New York (together with the American Academy of Arts and Letters); four works shown in exhibition of the work of grantees and newly elected members (May 23–June 24). Publishes *Fantasy Drawings* (with introduction by A. L. Chanin and essay by Samuel Atkin, M.D.). Is portrayed at work on wood and stone in educational 16 mm. film "The Sculptor Speaks," produced (in color, with sound) by Lewis Jacobs.

1957   *Sarah,* shown in 15th Annual Exhibition of Audubon Artists, Inc., New York, awarded honorable mention for sculpture. Works for a period of over four months in Rome (studio on the Via Margutta), executing works later cast by the Nicci art foundry. One-man exhibition (wood, stone, and bronze sculptures), Duveen Graham Gallery, New York. Publishes *The Technique of Wood Sculpture.* Travel: Athens, Istanbul, Israel.

1959   Represented (*Balancing*) in "American Painting and Sculpture," first cultural exchange exhibition prepared by Fine Arts Section of USIA as part of American National Exhibition, Moscow (July 25–September 5). Represented, by sculptures, drawings, and watercolors, in Whitney Museum of American Art retrospective exhibition "Four American Expressionists: Doris Caesar, Chaim Gross, Karl Knaths, Abraham Rattner" (January 14–March 1), which travels to New Hampshire, Colorado, Ohio, and Texas. Represented by three sculptures in "Art: USA: 59" exhibition held in New York Coliseum (April). Lives in Rome for several months, working in studio on Via Margutta; meets Severini, Fazzini, Emilio Greco, De Chirico, and other artists. Travel: Sicily, Amsterdam, Rotterdam, Israel, Paris.

1961   One-man exhibition (sculptures, drawings, and watercolors), Marble Arch Gallery, Miami Beach, Florida. Interviewed by Theodore Bikel on WABC TV program "Directions 61" (Sunday, April 30, 1:00 p.m., Channel 7).

1962   Represented in "Sculptors' Drawings from the Joseph H. Hirshhorn Collection," circulated by the National Collection of Fine Arts, Smithsonian Institution. One-man exhibitions (sculptures and drawings): Werbe Gallery, Detroit; Forum Gallery, New York (March 19–April 14).

1963   Receives Award of Merit (gold medal and prize of $1,000) for sculpture from the American Academy of Arts and Letters. Awarded first prize for sculpture *I Love My Baby*, Boston Arts Festival. One-man exhibition (sculpture, drawings, and watercolors), Irving Galleries, Milwaukee; sculpture and drawings, B'nai B'rith Building, Washington, D.C. (June 5–August 1). Represented (*Mimi Praying; Happy Mother*) in "Retrospective Art Exhibit of the Educational Alliance Art School," held at the American Federation of Arts Gallery, New York (April 29–May 18). Represented in second biennial exhibition "Drawings USA," Saint Paul Arts Center, St. Paul, Minnesota.

1964   One-man exhibitions: watercolors and drawings, Forum Gallery, New York (May 18–June 13); watercolors and drawings, Andrew Dickson White

72. The artist at work on THE HENNENFORDS ACROBATS. 1964

Museum of Art, Cornell University, Ithaca, New York. Represented in "Sculpture for Out of Doors," Birmingham Museum of Art (September 2–November 1). Elected to membership in the National Institute of Arts and Letters, New York. *Mother Playing* unveiled at Hadassah-Hebrew University Medical Center, Jerusalem. Travel: Paris, Rome, Israel.

1965   Receives Henry C. Avery Award, honorable mention, from the Architectural League of New York for the sculpture *Sisters*. *The Six Days of Creation*, six bronze bas-reliefs commissioned for the sanctuary of Temple Shaaray Tefila, New York, dedi-

73. The artist at work on plaster model of MENORAH WITH FIGURES, unique bronze (78 × 78″) for the "Goldman Park" garden of the Menorah Home and Hospital for the Aged and Infirm, Brooklyn, New York. 1965

74. The artist at work on plaster model of BIRDS OF PEACE (SEVEN MYSTIC BIRDS). 1965–66

cated September 17; on same day, retrospective exhibition of sculptures and watercolors opens at the temple, continuing to October 8. Executes *Menorah with Figures,* unique bronze, for the garden of the Menorah Home and Hospital for the Aged and Infirm, Brooklyn, New York. *Happy Mother* presented by Mr. and Mrs. Alexander Rittmaster to Albert Einstein College of Medicine of Yeshiva University, Bronx, New York, and placed in front of the Rose F. Kennedy Center for Research in Mental Retardation and Human Development. Travel: Mexico—Mexico City (especially the National Museum of Anthropology), Acapulco, Cuernavaca and neighboring villages.

1966   One-man exhibition (sculptures and drawings), Clark University, Worcester, Massachusetts. Executes *Birds of Peace* (also known as *Seven Mystic Birds*), unique bronze sculpture, for campus of the Hebrew University, Jerusalem. Travel: Peru—Lima, Cuzco, Machu Picchu.

1967   One-man exhibitions: Forum Gallery, New York (March 21–April 14); Carl Oestreicher Community Center, Temple Shaaray Tefila, New York (autumn); Wisconsin State University, Eau Claire. Interviewed by Leonard Harris on WCBS TV program "Gateway" (Saturday, October 7, 2:30 p. m., Channel 2), demonstrates modeling in clay, together with a group of his students from the New School for Social Research. Travel: Mexico—Yucatán, Uxmal, Chichén Itzá, Palenque, Villahermosa, Mexico City).

1968   Represented, by sculptures and drawings, in "Contemporary American Art: Check List of Opening Exhibition," National Collection of Fine Arts, Smithsonian Institution, Washington, D.C. (May–June). In Paris executes eleven original color lithographs for portfolio *The Jewish Holidays,* com-

75. The artist's studio, c. 1970. Foreground: GYROSCOPIC TWINS

missioned by Associated American Artists, New York, and printed in Paris in an edition of 250 suites. Travel: Israel, Venice, Florence, Rome, Paris.

1969   One-man exhibition (study drawings, original watercolors, and finished lithographs for portfolio *The Jewish Holidays*), Associated American Artists Galleries, New York. Receives commission from the New York Board of Rabbis for sculptures on the Ten Commandments for the sanctuary of the International Synagogue at John F. Kennedy International Airport, New York. One-man exhibitions: sculptures, drawings, and watercolors, Community Gallery of Lancaster County, Franklin and Marshall College, Lancaster, Pennsylvania (October 5–26); sculpture, lithographs, drawings, and watercolors, Phoenix Art

Museum (Hanukkah Festival, December 4–31). Travel: West Africa (Senegal, Bamako and other places in Mali, Accra, Kumasi, Abidjan, and fishing villages in Ghana), Madrid, Canary Islands.

1970 One-man exhibition (sculptures and watercolors), Medici II Gallery, Miami Beach, Florida (January 23–February 15). *I Love My Baby,* shown in 28th Annual Exhibition of Audubon Artists, Inc., New York, wins the President's Award for Sculpture. Receives honorary degree of Doctor of Fine Arts from Franklin and Marshall College, Lancaster, Pennsylvania.

1971 Travel: Barcelona, especially the Picasso Museum; the South of France (Aix-en-Provence, Arles, Bourges, Cannes, Nice, Antibes, especially the Picasso Museum), St. Paul de Vence (visit with Marc Chagall), Loire Valley, Avignon, Lyons, Paris.

1972 *The Ten Commandments,* commissioned for the sanctuary of the International Synagogue at Kennedy Airport, New York City, dedicated May 7. *The Performers,* commissioned for the Performing Arts Center of the University of Rhode Island is mounted in front of the Center. One-man exhibition (sculpture and watercolors), Forum Gallery, New York (March 24–April 14). Represented (*Tourists*) in "Humor, Satire, and Irony: An International Exhibition of Sculpture, Paintings, Drawings, and Prints," New School for Social Research, New York (October 25–December 19). *The Jewish Holidays,* book illustrated with the watercolors reproduced in the 1968 portfolio of lithographs, published by Forum Gallery, New York. Bronze sculpture *Happy Mother* purchased, in part by students, for The University Collections of Wichita State University, the first major outdoor sculpture on its campus (located in front of the main library).

76. THE PERFORMERS. 1972. Bronze, height 15' (22' with base). Fine Arts Center, University of Rhode Island, Kingston. Gift of Alice and Bo Bernstein

1973   Creates watercolor used as a cachet by the World Federation of United Nations Associations on the first-day cover put out to accompany the United Nations Commemorative stamp issue for Namibia (formerly known as South-West Africa). Completes maquette for 6-by-19-ft. stainedglass window on the theme of the Jewish Holy Days for Temple Emanu-El in Englewood, New Jersey. Published: *The Book of Isaiah: A New Translation, with Drawings by Chaim Gross* (Philadelphia, Jewish Publication Society of America). *Happy Children,* 6-ft. bronze sculpture, focal point of the Arrival Garden in the River City Mall, Louisville, unveiled, July 30. Revolving 6-ft. bronze sculpture *Happy Children* installed in new addition to the Cloverleaf Mall, Richmond, opened August 1.

1974   One-man exhibition (sculpture and drawings), National Collection of Fine Arts, Smithsonian Institution, Washington, D.C. (September 13–November 17). "Rebirth," a 6-by-19-ft. stained-glass window for Temple Emanu-el, Englewood, New Jersey, installed and dedicated, the artist's design having been realized by Jan Ooms, using a relatively new technique in which the stained-glass elements are combined not by lead but by being affixed to plate glass with an epoxy adhesive.

PLATES

77. The artist at work on 6-ft.
bronze sculpture HAPPY CHILDREN
for Cloverleaf Mall,
Richmond, Virginia. 1973

78. SKETCHES FOR SCULPTURE. 1929. Pen and ink, 12 × 19″. Collection the artist, New York City

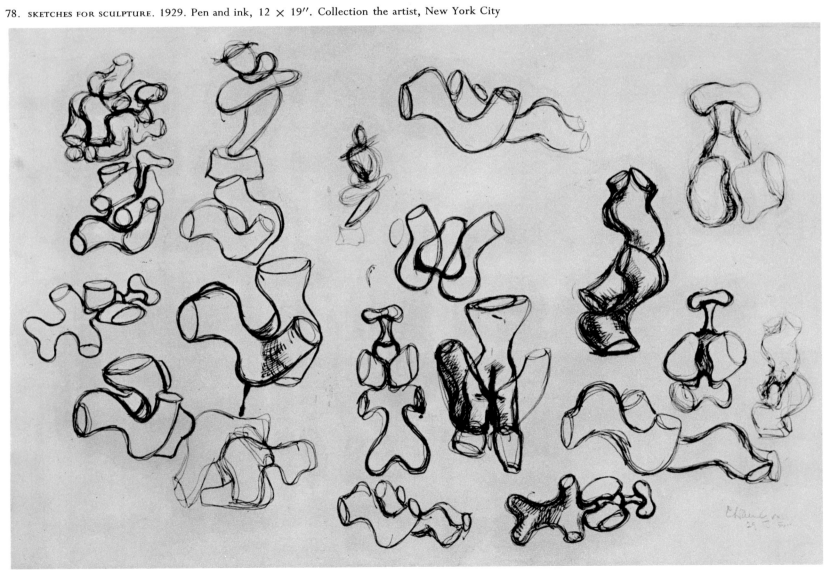

79. GIRL MAKING UP.
1929.
Lignum vitae, height 23".
Collection
Mr. and Mrs. A. Epstein,
New York City

80. CIRCUS GIRLS.
1932.
Ink, 18 × 12″.
Collection
Mimi Gross Grooms,
New York City

81. CIRCUS GIRLS.
1934.
Lignum vitae, height 36".
Collection
Mimi Gross Grooms,
New York City

82. ACROBATIC DANCE.
1933.
Mahogany, height 20".
Collection
the artist,
New York City

83. ROCK-A-BYE. 1935. Sepia wash, 15 × 21″. Collection the artist, New York City

84. Sketches for BIRD'S NEST.
    1934.
    Pencil, 13 × 18 1/2″.
    Collection the artist,
    New York City

85. SKETCHES FOR SCULPTURE.
    1935.
    Ink and sepia, 14 × 22 1/2″.
    Collection
    Mr. and Mrs. Samuel K. Gross,
    Roslyn Harbor, New York

86. SELF-PORTRAIT.
1933.
Walnut, height 17 1/4″.
Collection
Renee Nechin Gross,
New York City

opposite page, left:

87. HANDLEBAR RIDERS.
1935.
Lignum vitae, height 41 1/4″.
The Museum of Modern Art,
New York City.
Gift of A. Conger Goodyear

opposite page, right:

88. STRONG WOMAN.
1935.
Lignum vitae, height 48″.
Hirshhorn Museum
and Sculpture Garden,
Smithsonian Institution,
Washington, D.C.

89. MADAME.
1935.
Lignum vitae, height 21 3/4″.
Private collection,
New York City

90. AERIALIST. 1935. Sabicu wood, length 58 1/4". Forum Gallery, New York City

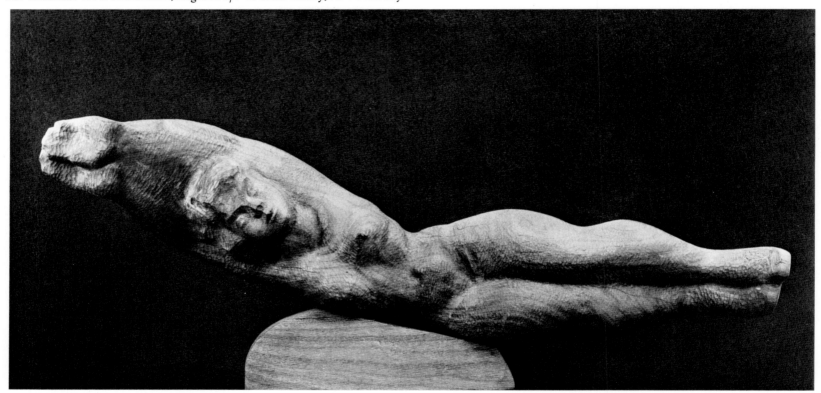

91. Study for HANDLEBAR RIDERS.
    1934.
    Blue-black ink and wash on buff paper,
    14 7/8 × 10 5/8″.
    The Museum of Modern Art, New York.
    Gift of the artist

92. MOTHER AND CHILD AT PLAY.
1937.
Palo blanco wood, height 56''.
The Newark Museum

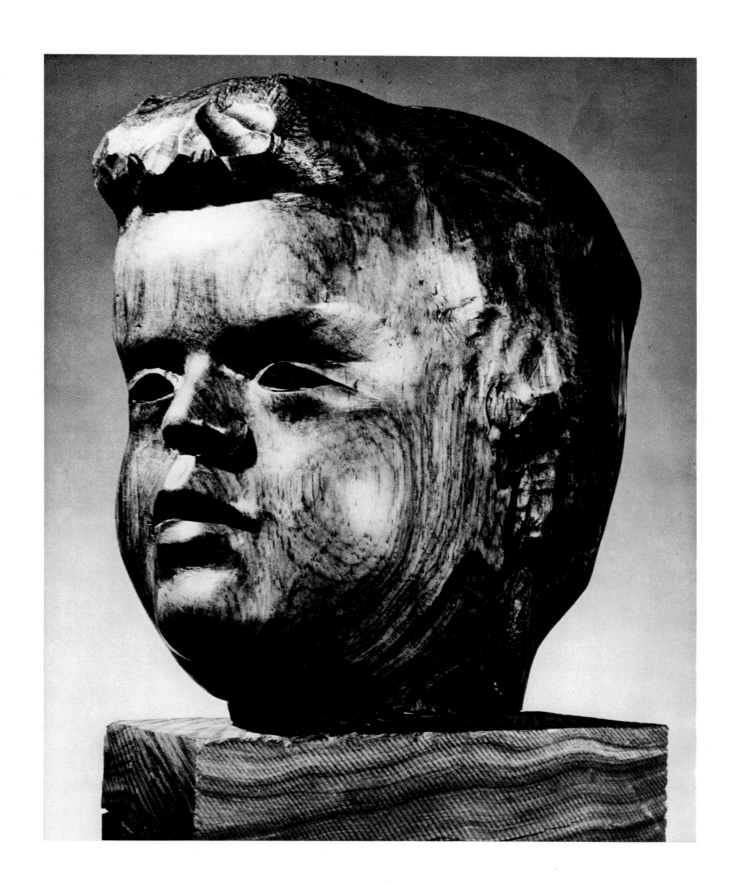

93. YEHUDAH ZACHARY GROSS.
    1937.
    Cocobolo wood, height 9″.
    Collection
    Mr. and Mrs. Saul Rosen,
    Paterson, New Jersey

94. ACROBATS BALANCING.
1938.
Lignum vitae, height 30″.
Collection
Renee Nechin Gross,
New York City

95. ACROBATS BALANCING
(detail)

96. FENCING BOY.
1937.
Ebony, height 40".
Queens College,
New York

97. HEAD OF RENEE.
1938.
Sabicu wood, height 25″.
Collection the artist,
New York City

98. AERIALIST.
1938.
Vermilion wood, height 53 1/2″.
Private collection,
New York City

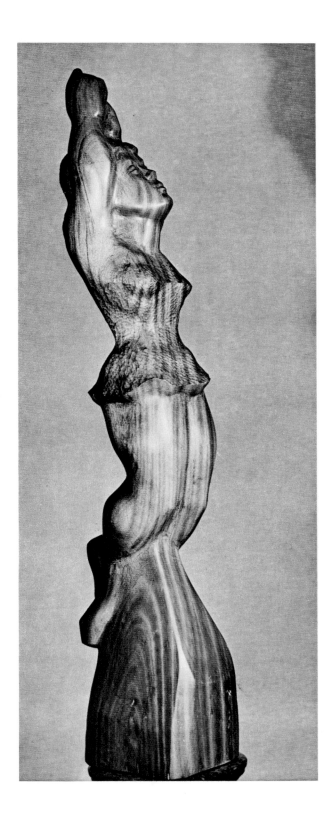

99. SKETCH FOR SCULPTURE. 1940. Sepia wash, 10 × 15″. Collection the artist, New York City

100. SKETCH FOR SCULPTURE.
   1940.
   Ink and watercolor, 20 × 13".
   Collection Mimi Gross Grooms,
   New York City

101. GIRL ON WHEEL: STATUETTE.
   1940.
   Lignum vitae, height 29".
   The Metropolitan Museum of Art, New York City.
   Morris K. Jesup Fund, 1942

102. SISTERS AT PLAY. 1942. Mexican onyx, height 26 1/2". Collection the artist, New York City

103. Study for VICTORIA.
1942.
Ink, 18 × 12″.
Collection the artist,
New York City

104. RENEE.
1944.
Italian black and gold marble,
height 23″.
Collection the artist,
New York City

105. TWINS.
1944.
Sabicu wood, 79 1/2 × 13″
Forum Gallery,
New York City

106. DEBORAH.
1945.
Italian pink marble, height 17″
Collection the artist,
New York City

107. SELF-PORTRAIT.
1945.
Ink, 15 × 10″.
Collection the artist,
New York City

108. ETERNAL MOTHER.
1945.
Lithium stone, height 28″.
Collection
Mimi Gross Grooms,
New York City

109. NAOMI.
1947.
Serpentine stone, height 29″.
Collection
Renee Nechin Gross,
New York City

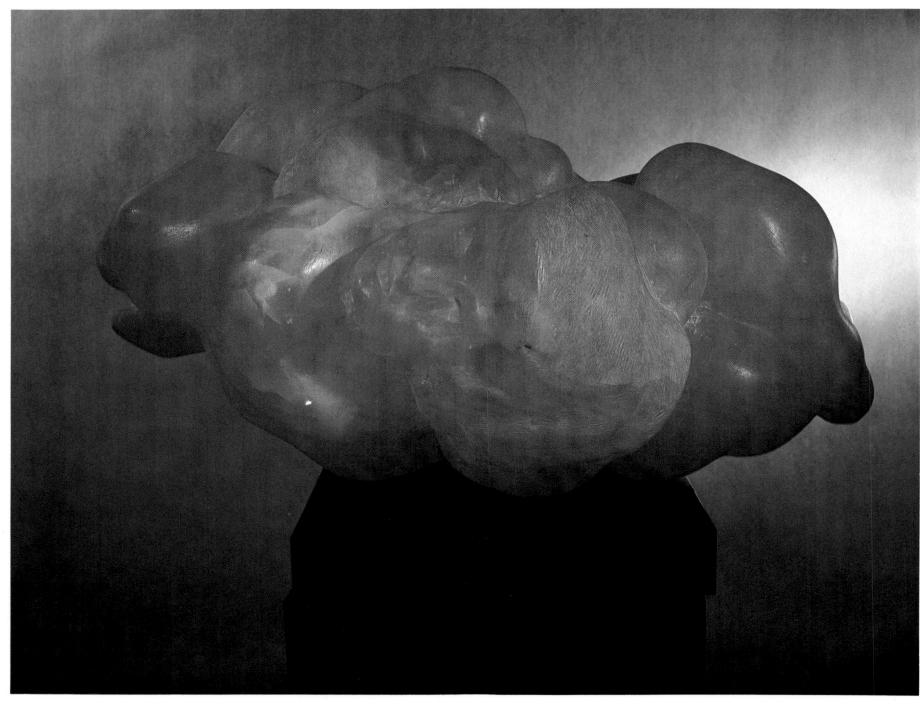

110. THE DREAM—ADOLESCENT ASLEEP. 1947. White alabaster, length 26". Collection the artist, New York City

111. UPSIDE DOWN.
1947.
Lignum vitae, height 11″.
Whereabouts unknown

112. IONE.
1948.
Pink alabaster, height 13 1/2″.
Collection
Mr. and Mrs. Max Drill,
South Orange, New Jersey

113. I FOUND MY LOVE.
1948.
Mexican tulipwood, height 78″.
Collection the artist,
New York City

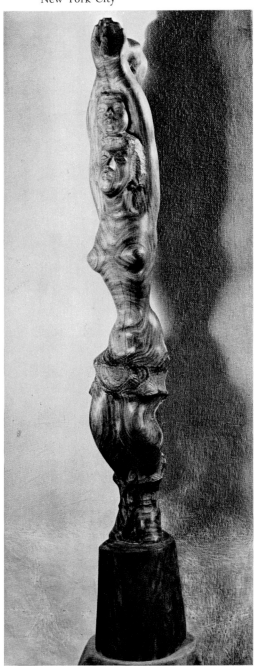

114. EASTER SUNDAY.
1948.
Lignum vitae, height 48 1/2″.
Collection
Renee Nechin Gross,
New York City

115. MOSES SOYER. 1970. Bronze, height 12″.
Forum Gallery, New York City

116. CHAIM WEIZMANN.
1949.
Bronze, height 21″.
Private collection,
New York City

117. I FOUND MY LOVE.
1949.
Polished bronze, height 78".
Collection
Lane Bryant, Inc.,
New York City

118. PRIDE.
    1949.
    Honduras mahogany, height 86″.
    Collection the artist,
    New York City

119. PLAYFUL SISTERS.
     1949.
     Mexican tulipwood,
     height 54″, base 14 × 11″.
     Hirshhorn Museum
     and Sculpture Garden,
     Smithsonian Institution, Washington, D.C.

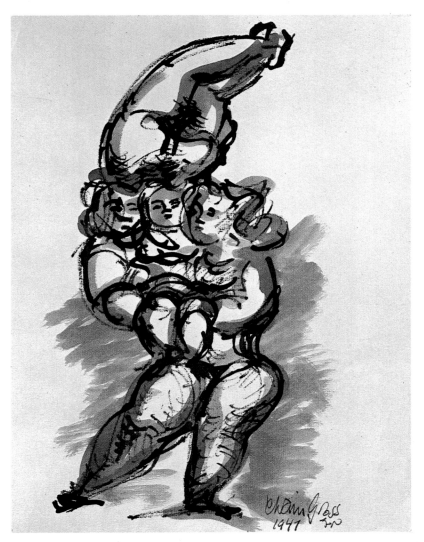

120. Sketch for PLAYFUL SISTERS. 1947. Ink and wash, 12 × 9″.
Collection Mr. and Mrs. Lawrence Richmond,
Great Neck, New York

121. BIRD'S NEST.
1949.
Bronze, height 66″.
Collection President,
40 Central Park South, Inc.,
New York City

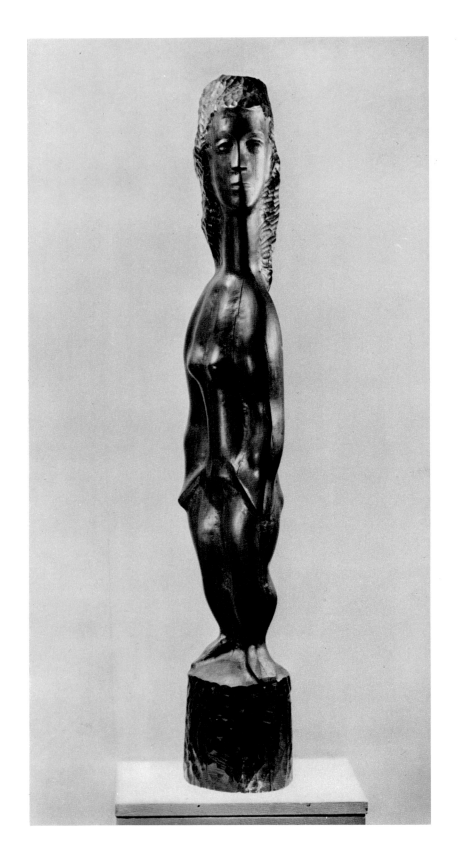

122. ADOLESCENT.
1950.
Ebony, height 41″, base 2 1/2″.
Philadelphia Museum of Art.
Given by
David A. Teichman, 1957

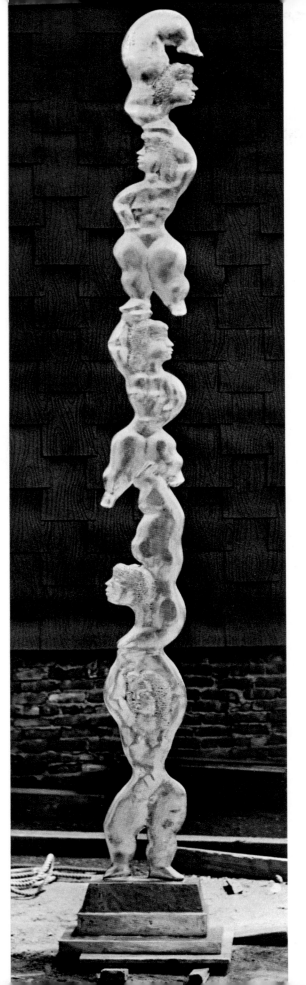

123. FAMILY OF FIVE.
    1951.
    Bronze, height 14 1/2".
    New School for Social Research,
    New York City.
    Donated by
    Mr. and Mrs. Harris J. Klein

124. FAMILY OF FIVE (detail)

125. ACROBATS PLAYING.
1951.
Lignum vitae, height 16".
Collection
Renee Nechin Gross,
New York City

126. PORTRAIT OF MIMI.
1952.
Bronze, height 15″.
Collection
Colonel Louis I.
and Mrs. Bessie K. Rosenfield,
Brookline, Massachusetts

127. ELAINE.
     1952.
     Pink alabaster, height 14″.
     Collection
     Mr. and Mrs. Ben Schanzer,
     New York City

128. JUMPING OVER.
    1952.
    Lignum vitae, 21 1/2 × 7″.
    Collection
    Mr. and Mrs. Herbert A. Steinmann,
    New York City

129. STANDING FIGURE.
    1952.
    Kingwood, height 13″.
    Dr. and Mrs. Alex H. Kaplan,
    St. Louis

130. TUMBLER.
1953.
Pink alabaster, 8 × 9″.
Collection
Mr. and Mrs. Harold Uris,
New York City

131. SKETCH FOR SCULPTURE. 1953. Pencil, 14 1/2 × 21″. Collection the artist, New York City

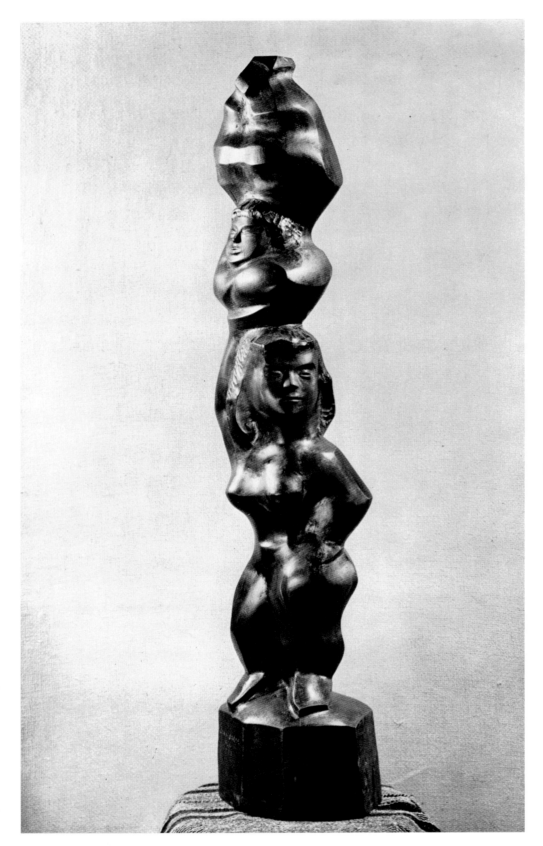

135. ACROBATS BALANCING.
1953.
Ebony, height 40".
Private collection,
Orlando, Florida

136. BALLERINA. 1953.
    Lignum vitae, height 23 1/2".
    Collection
    Mr. and Mrs. Solomon K. Gross,
    Roslyn, New York

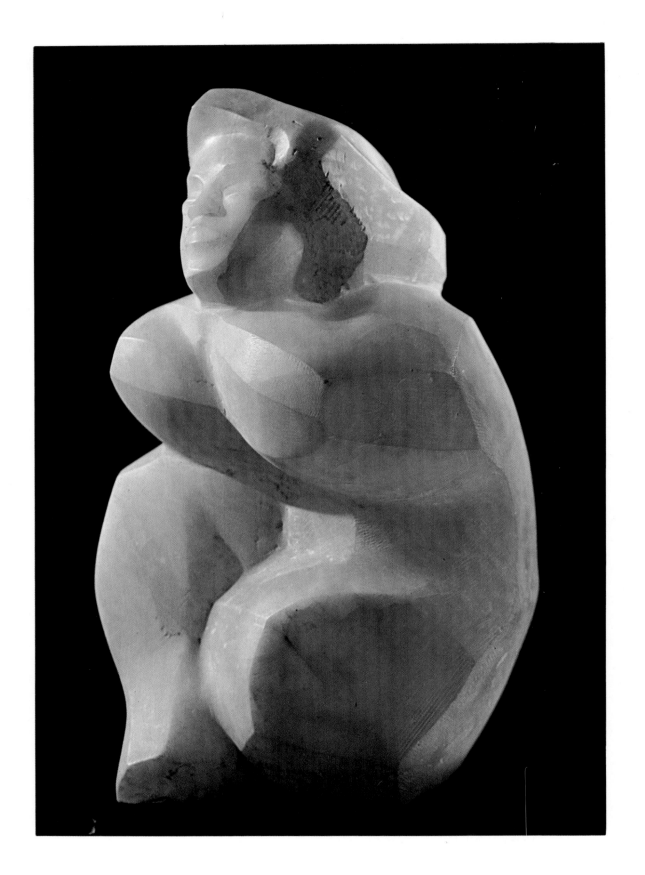

137. WAITING MOTHER.
1953.
White alabaster, height 27''.
Collection the artist,
New York City

138. SNAKE AND BIRDS.
1954.
Lignum vitae, height 60''.
Whitney Museum of American Art,
New York City

139. REFLECTION
(detail)

140. REFLECTION.
    1954.
    Pink alabaster, height 17″.
    Collection
    Mimi Gross Grooms,
    New York City

141. BALLERINAS.
1955.
Watercolor, 8 5/8 × 28″.
Collection the artist,
New York City

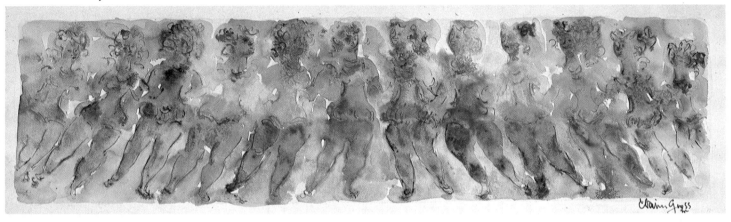

142. DANCERS. 1966. Watercolor, 8 5/8 × 34 5/8″. Collection the artist, New York City

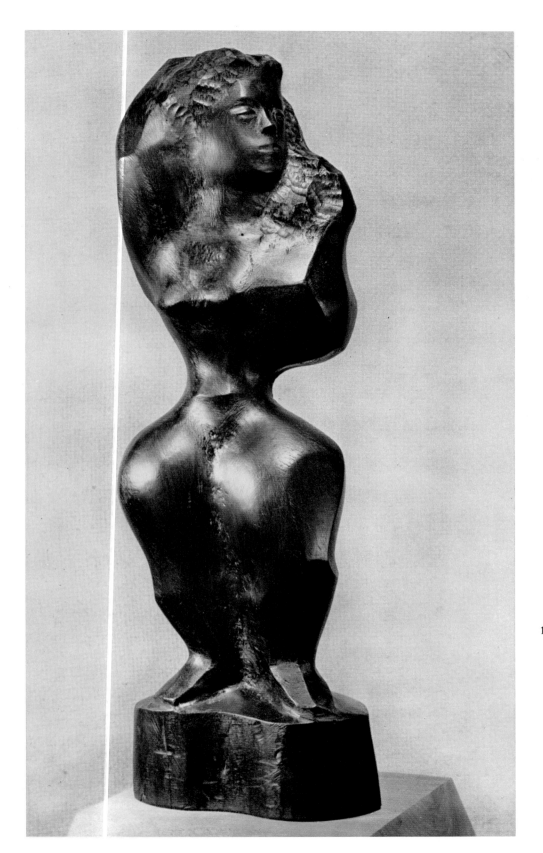

143. VANITY.
1955.
Ebony, height 20″.
Forum Gallery,
New York City

144. MIMI.
1955.
Belgian black marble, height 9″.
Collection
Mimi Gross Grooms,
New York City

145. YOUNG ACROBATS.
1955.
Ebony, height 49".
Forum Gallery,
New York City

146. MOTHER LEAH.
1956.
Lignum vitae, 37 × 10″.
Collection
Mr. and Mrs. Harris Klein,
Brooklyn, New York

147. RENEE.
1956.
Antique Italian marble,
height 17".
Collection the artist,
New York City

148. HEADSTAND.
   1956.
   Serpentine stone, 12 × 16″.
   Collection
   Bernard Osher, Biddeford,
   Maine

149. SEATED FIGURE.
1956.
Serpentine stone, 10 × 12″.
Collection
Mr. and Mrs. Saul Rosen,
Paterson, New Jersey

150. MOTHER PLAYING WITH TWO CHILDREN (detail)

151. MOTHER PLAYING WITH TWO CHILDREN. 1957. Bronze, length 24″. Kalamazoo Institute of Arts, Michigan

152. MOTHER DANCING.
    1957.
    Bronze, height 10″.
    Collection
    Mr. and Mrs. Herbert A. Goldstone,
    New York City

153. BABY BALANCING.
1957.
Bronze, 12 × 11".
Collection
Mr. and Mrs. Nathan Straus III,
New York City

154. THREE ACROBATS ON A UNICYCLE.
1957.
Bronze, height 78″.
National Collection of Fine Arts,
Smithsonian Institution,
Washington, D.C.

155. DANCING GIRLS.
1958.
Bronze, height 12″.
Collection
Mr. and Mrs. Leonard Zahn,
Kings Point, New York

156. FLYING TRAPEZE (back view).
1958.
Bronze, 15 1/2 × 13".
Collection
Mr. and Mrs. Gerard Oestreicher,
New York City

157. FLYING TRAPEZE (front view).

158. HAPPY MOTHER. 1958. Bronze, length 90″. Albert Einstein College of Medicine of Yeshiva University, New York City

159. HAPPY MOTHER. 1958. Bronze, 11 × 13″. Collection Dr. and Mrs. Jacob Begner, New York City

160. JUGGLER.
1959.
Bronze, 24 × 22″.
Collection
Mr. and Mrs. Eugene R. Steinberg,
Great Neck, New York

161. THE MARKET IN JERUSALEM. 1958. Watercolor and ink, 22 1/2 × 31 1/4″. Collection the artist, New York City

162. TWO RING PERFORMERS.
1959.
Bronze, 41 × 22″.
Collection
George Hofrichter,
New York City

163. HANDSTAND.
1959.
Bronze, 25 1/2 × 14″.
Collection
Joseph N. Attie,
Great Neck, New York

164. ACROBATIC DANCERS.
1959.
Bronze, height 16 1/2″ with
pedestal base
(12 3/4″ without base).
Collection
Mr. and Mrs. Myron A. Minskoff,
New York City

165. TOURISTS.
1959.
Bronze, height 66".
Chrysler Museum at Norfolk

166. Sketch for BAREBACK RIDERS. 1960. Pencil, 11 1/2 × 27 1/2″. Collection Mr. and Mrs. Mac Rabinowitz, Brooklyn, New York

167. BAREBACK RIDERS.
1960.
Bronze, 24 × 28″.
Collection
Mr. and Mrs. Morton L. Polk,
Westport, Connecticut

168. DRAWING (UNTITLED). 1960. India ink and watercolor, 10 3/4 × 14″. Collection Mr. and Mrs. Paul Anbinder, Dobbs Ferry, New York

169. BALLERINAS.
1960.
Bronze, 10 × 30".
Collection Mr. and Mrs. David A. Wingate,
East Hills, New York

170. MOTHER LOVE.
1960.
Pink alabaster, 14 1/2 × 11″.
Collection
Mr. and Mrs. Mac Rabinowitz,
Brooklyn, New York

171. JUDITH.
   1960.
   Rosewood, 10 3/4 × 7 1/8 × 2 1/2″.
   National Collection of Fine Arts,
   Smithsonian Institution, Washington, D.C.
   Gift of the artist

172. ZAHOVA.
1960.
Gray alabaster, height 14″.
Collection
Alice and Bo Bernstein,
Providence, Rhode Island

173. NEWBORN.
1960.
Gray alabaster, height 14″.
Whereabouts unknown

174. MOTHER PLAYING (front view).
1961.
Bronze, 48 × 80".
Hadassah-Hebrew University Medical Center,
Jerusalem.
Gift of Mr. and Mrs. Morris Primoff,
New York City.

175. MOTHER PLAYING (back view).

176. SKETCH FOR SCULPTURE.
1961.
Sepia wash, 19 5/8 × 12 3/4″.
Collection the artist,
New York City

177. SEGOVIA.
1961.
Bronze, height 14″.
Collection
Mr. and Mrs. Miles Rubin,
Malibu, California

178. HOMAGE TO MARC CHAGALL.
1961.
Bronze, 10 × 16".
Collection
Mr. and Mrs. Harold J. Ruttenberg,
Pittsburgh and Jerusalem

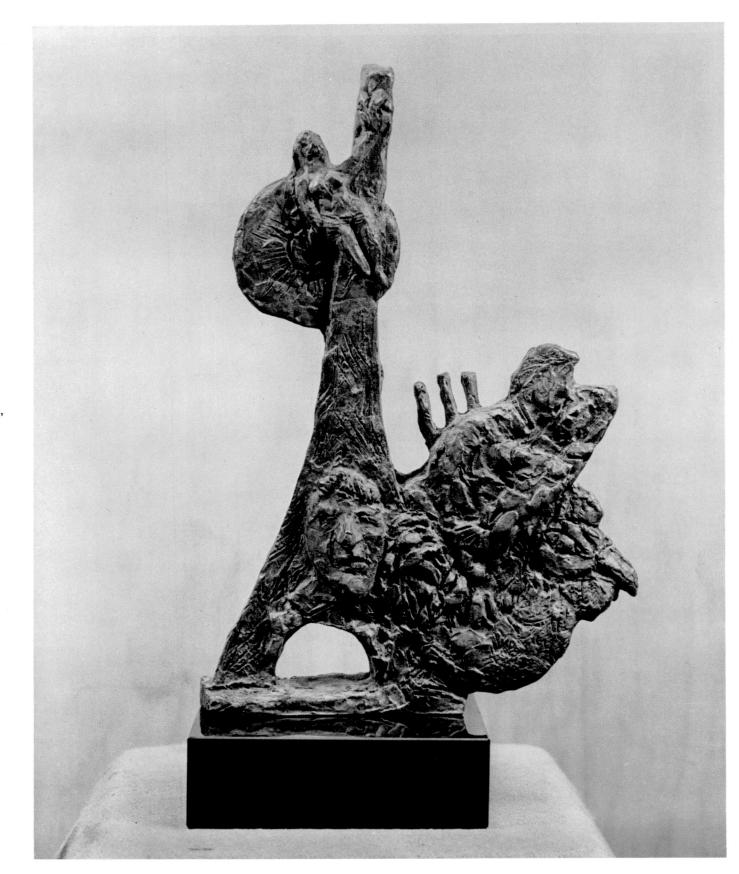

179. HOMAGE TO MARC CHAGALL.
1961.
Bronze, 10 × 6″.
Collection
Alice and Bo Bernstein,
Providence, Rhode Island

180. HOMAGE TO MARC CHAGALL.
1962.
Bronze, 36 × 22″.
Collection
Mr. and Mrs. Lawrence Richmond,
Great Neck, New York

181. BALLET "SYMPHONY IN C"
   (one of three panels).
   1962.
   Bronze, 30 × 20".
   Forum Gallery,
   New York City

182. TIGHTROPE ACROBATS.
1962.
Bronze, height 84″.
Forum Gallery,
New York City

183. SKETCH FOR SCULPTURE.
1962.
Pencil, 14 × 11″.
Collection
Alice and Bo Bernstein,
Providence, Rhode Island

184. ACROBATS. 1962. Ink and pencil, 13 1/8 × 20 1/8″. Collection Alice and Bo Bernstein, Providence, Rhode Island

185. MOTHER AND BABY ROCKING.
1962.
Bronze, 16 × 12″.
Collection
Mr. and Mrs. Norman B. Robbins,
Worcester, Massachusetts

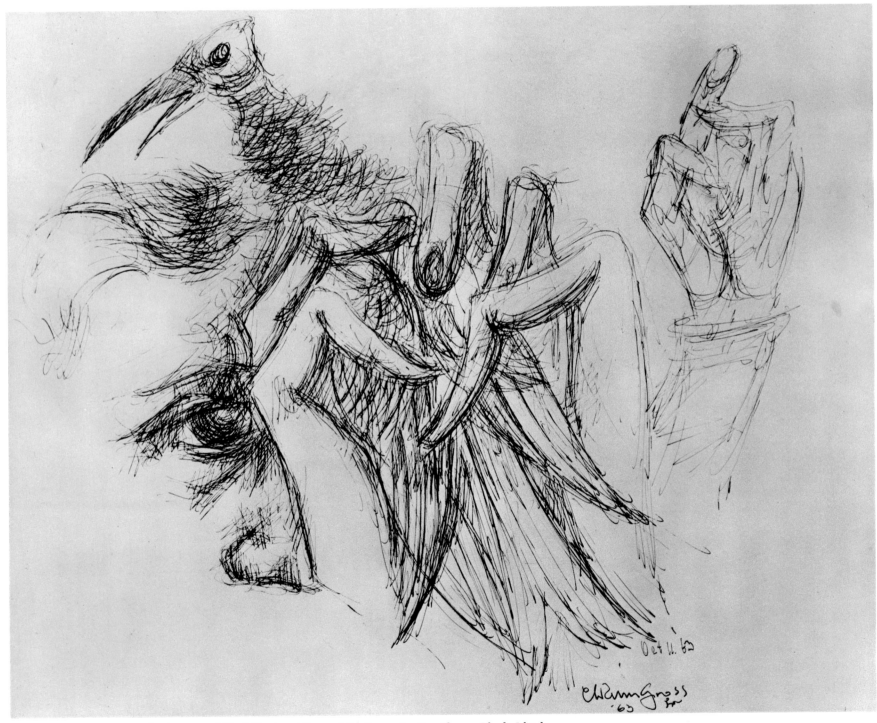

186. FANTASY. 1963. Pen and ink, 14 × 17″. Collection Alice and Bo Bernstein, Providence, Rhode Island

187. VANITY.
1963.
Bronze, height 14″.
Collection Gisèle Allard,
New York City

188. ACROBAT IN THE RING #2.
1963.
Bronze, height 13″.
Collection
Mr. and Mrs. Lester Greenwald,
Larchmont, New York

189. HANDSTAND #3.
1963.
Bronze, 15 1/2 × 12″.
Collection
Mr. and Mrs. Peter Morrison,
New York City

190. RECLINING FIGURE. 1964. Pink alabaster, length 10″. Whereabouts unknown

191. PERFORMER.
1963.
Bronze, height 14 1/2".
Collection
Dr. and Mrs. Alvin J. Feldman,
New York City

192. THE DANCE.
1963.
Bronze, height 27".
Collection
Mr. and Mrs. Joseph Kahn,
New York City

193. MENORAH WITH FIGURES.
1964.
Welded bronze and metal, 36 × 39″.
Collection the artist,
New York City

194. STUDY OF NUDE #1.
    1964.
    Sepia wash and pencil, 20 × 11″.
    Collection
    Renee Nechin Gross,
    New York City

195. STUDY OF NUDE #2.
    1964.
    Sepia wash and pencil, 20 × 11″.
    Collection
    Renee Nechin Gross,
    New York City

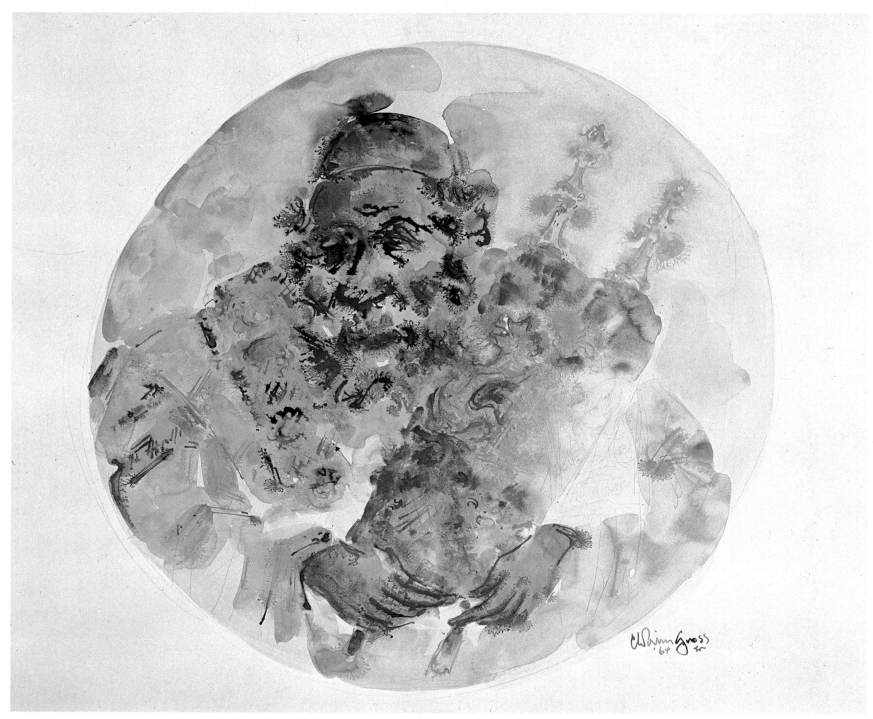

196. IN FRONT OF THE ARK. 1964. Watercolor, 22 7/8 × 29 1/4″. Collection the artist, New York City

197. DAVID AND JOSEPH LIEBER
(grandsons of Raphael Soyer).
1969.
Bronze, 12 × 12″.
Collection Rebecca and Raphael Soyer,
New York City

198. ACROBATS THROUGH THE RING.
1964.
Bronze, 36 × 15″.
Collection
Mr. and Mrs. Jack Baron,
Great Neck, New York

199. THE HENNENFORDS ACROBATS.
1964.
Bronze, height 90″.
Collection the artist,
New York City

200. PERFORMER.
1964.
Pencil, 20 1/2 × 11".
Collection the artist,
New York City

201. TRAPEZE PERFORMERS.
1964.
Bronze, 19 × 21 1/2".
Collection
Alice and Bo Bernstein,
Providence, Rhode Island

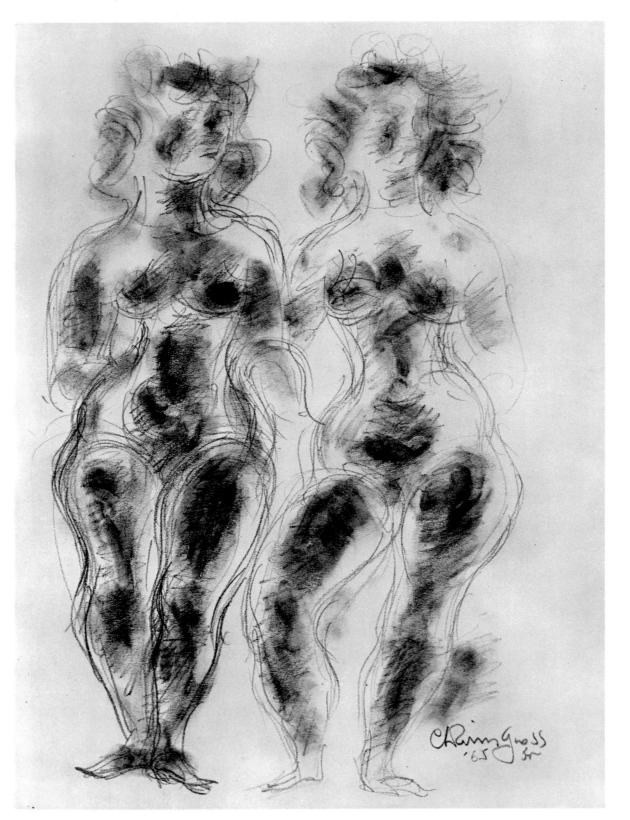

202. STUDY FROM THE FIGURE.
1965.
Pencil, 15 × 11".
Collection the artist,
New York City

203. NAOMI AND RUTH.
1965. Lithium stone, height 10″.
Collection
Mr. and Mrs. Lawrence Richmond,
Great Neck, New York

204. ARLENE.
1965.
Black alabaster, 10 × 6″.
Collection the artist,
New York City

205. Sketch for BIRDS OF PEACE
(SEVEN MYSTIC BIRDS).
1964.
Wash and ink, 18 × 13″.
Collection the artist,
New York City

206. BIRDS OF PEACE (SEVEN MYSTIC BIRDS).
1966.
Unique bronze, 99 × 48″.
Hebrew University, Jerusalem

207. I LOVE MY BABY. 1965. Sepia wash and pencil, 11 × 20 3/8″. Collection Mimi Gross Grooms, New York City

208. ACROBATS THROUGH THE RING.
1966.
Pencil, 13 × 8″.
Collection the artist,
New York City

209. SKETCH FOR SCULPTURE MONUMENT #2.
1966.
Bronze 27 × 12″.
Collection the artist,
New York City

210. MAGDALENE. 1965. Pink alabaster, 11 1/2 × 16″. Collection Renee Nechin Gross, New York City

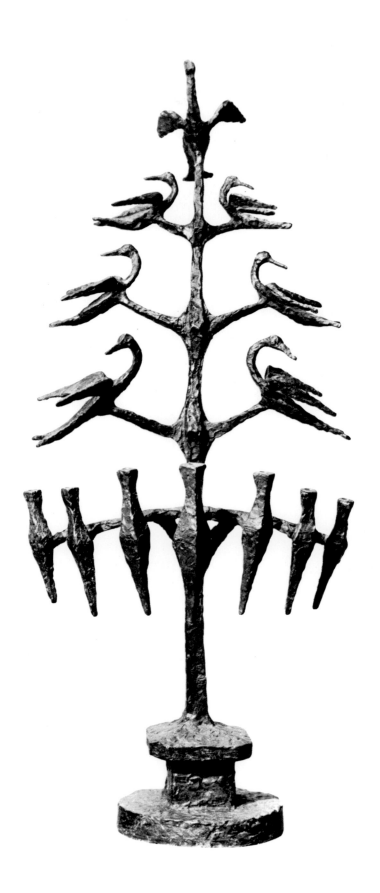

211. MENORAH WITH SEVEN BIRDS.
1966.
Bronze, 60 × 19″.
Collection the artist,
New York City

212. BALLERINAS #2.
1966.
Bronze, 15 × 14″.
Collection
Judith and Meshulam Riklis,
New York City

213. JUGGLER.
1966.
Bronze, 24 × 12″.
Collection
Mr. and Mrs. Benjamin M. Ganeles,
Mt. Vernon, New York

214. POETESS.
1966.
Pink alabaster, 11 × 7″.
Collection Red Grooms,
New York City

215. FIRST DAY, "THE SIX DAYS OF CREATION."
1964–66.
Bronze, height 9'6".
Temple Shaaray Tefila,
New York City

216. SECOND DAY, "THE SIX DAYS
OF CREATION."
1964–66.
Bronze, height 9'6".
Temple Shaaray Tefila,
New York City

217. THIRD DAY, "THE SIX DAYS OF CREATION."
1964–66.
Bronze, height 9'6".
Temple Shaaray Tefila, New York City

218. FOURTH DAY, "THE SIX DAYS
OF CREATION."
1964–66.
Bronze, height 9'6".
Temple Shaaray Tefila,
New York City

219. FIFTH DAY, "THE SIX DAYS
OF CREATION."
1964–66.
Bronze, height 9'6".
Temple Shaaray Tefila,
New York City

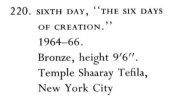

220. SIXTH DAY, "THE SIX DAYS
OF CREATION."
1964–66.
Bronze, height 9'6".
Temple Shaaray Tefila,
New York City

221. Sketch for ETERNAL MOTHER #3.
1966.
Bronze, height 16 1/2″.
Collection
Mr. and Mrs. Sidney E. Cohn,
New York City

222. DANCE RHYTHM.
1966.
Bronze, height 87″.
Collection
Mr. and Mrs. Lawrence Richmond,
Great Neck, New York

223. SKETCH FOR SCULPTURE MONUMENT #1.
1966.
Bronze, 27 1/2 × 12″.
Collection the artist,
New York City

224. MATERNAL AFFECTION #2.
1966.
Bronze, height 41 1/2".
Collection
Judith and Meshulam Riklis,
New York City

225. PORTRAIT OF KARL KNATHS.
1967.
Bronze, height 15".
Syracuse University Art Collection,
New York

226. ETERNAL MOTHER.
1967.
Bronze, height 62 1/2".
Forum Gallery,
New York City

231. ETERNAL MOTHER
(detail)

232. BALANCING. 1967. Pencil, 11 3/4 × 29″. Collection the artist, New York City

233. MENORAH.
1972.
Bronze, 45 × 22 1/2 × 14″.
Forum Gallery,
New York City

234. MENORAH WITH BIRDS.
1968.
Bronze, 90 × 45 × 29″.
Temple Sinai, Pittsburgh.
Gift of Mr. and Mrs. Harold Ruttenberg

235. SHABBAT—MENORAH
1973.
Bronze, 39 × 39 × 15″.
Forum Gallery,
New York City

236. HAPPY CHILDREN (and detail).
1968.
Bronze, 72 × 24 × 24″.
Forum Gallery,
New York City

241. TEN COMMANDMENTS.
 1970–71.
 International Synagogue,
 John F. Kennedy International Airport,
 New York City.
 Bronze plaques, each 30 × 42″,
 mounted on a wood panel

242. FIRST COMMANDMENT: "Thou shalt have no other gods before me."

243. SECOND COMMANDMENT: "Thou shalt not make unto thee any graven image. . . ."

244. THIRD COMMANDMENT: "Thou shalt not take the name of the LORD thy GOD in vain. . . ."

245. FOURTH COMMANDMENT: "Remember the sabbath day, to keep it holy."

246. FIFTH COMMANDMENT: ''Honor thy father and thy mother.''

247. SIXTH COMMANDMENT: ''Thou shalt not kill.''

248. SEVENTH COMMANDMENT: "Thou shalt not commit adultery."

249. EIGHTH COMMANDMENT: "Thou shalt not steal."

250. NINTH COMMANDMENT: "Thou shalt not bear false witness against thy neighbor."

251. TENTH COMMANDMENT: ''Thou shalt not covet thy neighbor's house . . . nor anything that is thy neighbor's.''

SELECTED BIBLIOGRAPHY

BY THE ARTIST

Writings

"A Sculptor's Progress," *Magazine of Art,* vol. 31, no. 12 (December 1938), pp. 694–98.

Fantasy Drawings, with introduction by A. L. Chanin, analytical essay by Samuel Atkin, M.D. New York: Beechhurst Press, 1956.

The Technique of Wood Sculpture. New York: Vista House, 1957; 2nd printing, Arco Publishing Company, 1966.

Sculpture in Progress (with Peter Robinson). New York: Van Nostrand-Reinhold, 1972.

Illustrated Books

Gross, Naftoli, *Mayses* (*Tales*). New York: Posy Shulson Press, 1935. (In Yiddish.)

————, *Mayselekh un mesholim* (*Tales and Parables*). New York: Aber Press, 1955. (In Yiddish.)

Soltes, Avraham, *The Jewish Holidays: Watercolors by Chaim Gross.* New York: Forum Gallery, 1972.

The Book of Isaiah: A New Translation, with Drawings by Chaim Gross. Philadelphia: The Jewish Publication Society of America, 1973.

ABOUT THE ARTIST

"Before 160,000 Eyes," *The Art Digest,* vol. 15, no. 1 (October 1, 1940), p. 14.

Benson, E. M., "Exhibition Reviews: Ahron Ben-Shmuel and Chaim Gross at the Guild Gallery," *The American Magazine of Art,* vol. 29, no. 1 (January 1936), pp. 39–41.

"Chaim Gross," *Current Biography*. New York: The H. W. Wilson Company, 1941, pp. 351–52.

Craven, Wayne, *Sculpture in America*. New York: Thomas Y. Crowell Company, 1968, pp. 586–88, 609.

D[avidson], M[artha], "New Exhibitions of the Week: Chaim Gross," *Art News,* vol. 35, no. 20 (February 13, 1937), p. 18.

Devree, Howard, "Seeing the Shows: Chaim Gross," *Magazine of Art,* vol. 30, no. 3 (March 1937), pp. 176–77.

Farber, Manny, "Chaim Gross, Milton Avery, and William Steig," *The Magazine of Art,* vol. 36, no. 1 (January 1943), pp. 10–15 and cover.

"Good Humor in Bronze," *Time,* vol. 79, no. 14 (April 6, 1962), pp. 66, 69.

Goodrich, Lloyd, and Baur, John I. H., *Four American Expressionists: Doris Caesar, Chaim Gross, Karl Knaths, Abraham Rattner* (exhibition catalogue). New York: Frederick A. Praeger for the Whitney Museum of American Art, 1959.

"Gross, Wood Carver," *Art Digest,* vol. 11, no. 10 (February 15, 1937), p. 20.

"Happy Sculptor," *Time,* vol. 69, no. 17 (April 29, 1957), p. 76.

K[ayser], S[tephen], "Introduction," in *Chaim Gross: Exhibition* (exhibition catalogue). New York: The Jewish Museum, 1953.

Lombardo, Josef Vincent, *Chaim Gross, Sculptor*. New York: Dalton House, Inc., 1949.

Reed, Judith Kaye, "Sculpture by Gross," *Art Digest,* vol. 22, no. 3 (November 1, 1947), p. 14.

"Reviews & Previews: Chaim Gross," *Art News,* vol. 46, no. 9, part 1 (November 1947), p. 43.

Schack, William, "Four Vital Sculptors," *Parnassus,* vol. 9, no. 2 (February 1937), pp. 12–14, 40.

Shelley, Melvin Geer, "Around the Galleries: Gallery 144 West 13th Street," *Creative Art,* vol. 10, no. 3 (April 1932), p. 304.

"Supple Sculpture: Chaim Gross Makes Lively Figures of Lithe Nudes and Agile Acrobats," *Life,* vol. 30, no. 2 (January 8, 1951), pp. 64–67.

"Tree Trunk to Head," *Magazine of Art,* vol. 31, no. 12 (December 1938), p. 716.

Werner, Alfred, "The Draftsmanship of Chaim Gross," in *The Book of Isaiah: A New Translation, with Drawings by Chaim Gross*. Philadelphia: The Jewish Publication Society of America, 1973, pp. 27–29.

Wolf, Ben, "Watercolors by Gross," *Art Digest,* vol. 20, no. 9 (February 1, 1946), p. 11.

ON WOOD CARVING

Davis, L. R., "American Wood Sculpture," *The Studio,* vol. 108, no. 501 (December 1934), pp. 278–81.

Durst, Alan L., *Wood Carving.* London and New York: Studio Publications, 1938

Harris, Ruth Green, and Piccoli, Girolamo, *Techniques of Sculpture.* New York: Harper & Brothers, 1942.

Hepworth, Barbara, "Approach to Sculpture," *The Studio,* vol. 132, no. 643 (October 1946), pp. 97–101.

Hoffman, Malvina, *Sculpture Inside and Out.* New York: W. W. Norton and Company, 1939.

Krasnow, Peter, "An Approach to Wood Sculpture," *California Arts & Architecture,* January 1944, pp. 18–19, 40, 46.

Miller, Alec, "Sculpture in Wood," *The American Magazine of Art,* vol. 21, no. 6 (June 1930), pp. 329–34.

Rich, Jack C., *Sculpture in Wood.* New York: Oxford University Press, 1970.

PHOTO CREDITS